AN ABRIDGED HISTORY
OF CATHOLIC CAMPUS MINISTRY

By
Fr. Albert Felice-Pace, O.P., S.T.L., M.A.

Foreword by
Most Rev. Phillip Straling, D.D.

To Jim Caruso

Fr. Albert Felice-Pace, OP

This book is dedicated to all campus ministers from the Western Dominican Province, and all the sisters and laity who ministered with them. Thank you to all of the provincials who saw this ministry as a vital one in the church.

The cover was designed by Johnson Shao,
an alumnus of the University of Nevada-Las Vegas
and a Newman Center alumnus.
It depicts Fr. Albert Felice-Pace, O.P.,
leading students in the Stations of the Cross
on the University of Oregon campus in 1989.

ISBN: 978-0-615-73558-0

FOREWORD

Most Reverend Phillip Straling, D.D.

When Fr. Albert Felice-Pace, O.P., was asked by his superior to serve as Newman Club chaplain, he had the same question I asked of my bishop: "What is a Newman Club?" All of my education up to being ordained a priest in 1959 had been in Catholic schools and seminary. This is what was expected of a good Catholic. So being asked to step onto San Diego State College (later a university) as a campus chaplain, I was going to unknown and forbidden territory. It so happened that at the very time of my being appointed to serve as chaplain at State College, Charles Francis Buddy, Bishop of the Diocese of San Diego, had just built and opened a Catholic University—the University of San Diego. Thankfully a number of people convinced the bishop that not all students could or were able to attend the new University of San Diego, reminding him students and faculty on other campuses also needed pastoral care and services. Listening to their advice, Bishop Buddy called me in 1961, appointing me part time to campus ministry at San Diego State and part time as an associate at a nearby parish.

When I asked what the task of a campus chaplain was, I remember the bishop saying to me, "You will do well!" which did not answer my question. In making arrangements with the administration at San Diego State to serve as a chaplain on campus, I was given a parking spot for my car in the visitor parking lot—a clue to my official status on campus. To explore my ministry I began having meetings with students and faculty in available classrooms during lunch or free time. Later I convinced the bishop to purchase a house near campus to serve as a Newman Center. Another way I found to become a part of campus life was to become a student myself, taking classes to obtain a Master of Science degree in counseling and getting a California state license as a family and marriage counselor. Little by little, with the help from the various sources outlined in Fr. Felice-Pace's *An Abridged History of Campus Ministry*, I found my role and ministry as a campus chaplain on a secular campus.

A couple of years after beginning as a campus minister I convinced Bishop Buddy to release me from all parish responsibilities to work full time in campus ministry. I was given the additional task of serving as the diocesan director of campus ministry with the responsibility of establishing programs on the other state and city campuses in the Diocese of San Diego. This how I met and worked with Fr. Albert Felice-Pace, O.P., because the Dominican community agreed to provide chaplains to serve the University of California-Riverside. The Paulist Fathers came to serve at the University of California at San Diego. Then, I persuaded priests in nearby parishes to serve as chaplains at other colleges and universities in the diocese.

My work in campus ministry concluded in 1972, when I was asked to lead a diocesan synod. What I learned from being a Newman chaplain has remained an important part of my formation as a parish priest and later bishop. My training and work prior to my becoming a campus chaplain had been in the pre-Vatican II church. My years in campus ministry included the time prior, during, and after Vatican II. When I was appointed the founding bishop of the new Diocese of San Bernardino in 1978, I had to create a coat of arms not only for the new diocese but also a coat of arms to represent me as the bishop. In drawing up the personal coat of arms, I chose the three hearts and the "Cor ad Cor Loquitur" of Blessed John Henry Cardinal Newman, representing my ministry as a campus chaplain.

An Abridged History of Campus Ministry compiled by Fr. Albert Felice-Pace, O.P., provides the large picture of campus ministry, outlining a response to a need, growth, challenge and maturity to help serve students and faculty on non-Catholic, secular colleges and universities. My work and ministry of twelve years was but a small part of a much larger work. All of us who are or were in this ministry treasure our part. This history also sets campus ministry side by side with the Church's other major ministries and works. Those attending these colleges and universities will find the church there to serve. *An Abridged History of Campus Ministry* provides help to one who asks the question: "What is a Newman Club?"

Most Reverend Phillip Straling, D.D.
Bishop Emeritus, Reno
Former Campus Minister
May 11, 2012

WHO AM I?
Introduction of Fr. Albert Robert Felice-Pace, O.P.

I was born in Malta, a small island in the middle of the Mediterranean Sea. According to the first verse of Chapter 28 of the Acts of the Apostles, St. Paul was shipwrecked on the island. As the third child of seven children, I attended my home elementary school and then the government public high school called The Lyceum. A year after I finished high school, I entered the Dominican Order. After finishing my classes in philosophy and theology, I earned the Lector of Sacred Theology degree in philosophy and theology. I was ordained to the priesthood on April 2, 1960. A year and a half after my ordination, I was asked to minister in the Western Dominican Province of the United States. I came to this country in November 1961. I also attended the University of San Francisco where I earned a Master of Arts in Adult Religious Education.

When I came to the Western Province, I was assigned as Associate Pastor at St. Mary Magdalen in Berkeley, California. After one year in Berkeley, I was assigned to St. Dominic Parish in Los Angeles as Associate Pastor and Newman Chaplain at Occidental College.

After seven years in Los Angeles, I was appointed Student Master (director of our seminarians) at St. Albert's Priory in Oakland, California. After serving two years as Student Master and a one-year sabbatical, I moved to the Newman community at the University of California, Riverside. After serving the Newman community for four years, I was appointed Director of Adult Education and the Charismatic Renewal, first for the north counties of the Diocese of San Diego and later for the new Diocese of San Bernardino.

In 1980 I returned to campus ministry. I was appointed Director at All Saints Catholic Newman Community serving Arizona State University in Tempe, Arizona. I have been in campus ministry ever since. After Arizona State University, I served at the University of Oregon in Eugene, Oregon; The University of Arizona in Tucson, Arizona; and now the University of Nevada Las Vegas.

Besides serving various Newman communities, I decided to get involved in the national, regional, and local levels. While in Eugene, I helped to establish the Pacific Northwest Catholic Campus Ministry Association (PNCCMA). I was elected its first president. For six years I was elected as the Western representative on the CCMA Executive Board, and for four years I served on the national executive committee of the Diocesan Directors of Catholic Campus Ministry. I served also on various committees of our association. In 1992 I chaired the national conference, which took place in San Jose, California. For three years I directed the Frank J. Lewis Institute for new campus ministers at the University of San Francisco. During my involvement in various national events and boards, I was elected to serve as a member of the Western Dominican Province Provincial Council. I had my plate pretty full—but I believed in giving.

On January 7, 1985, I was awarded the "Reverend Charles Forsyth Award" in recognition for leadership in campus ministry nationally, regionally, and locally. On January 3, 2003, I was recognized by the National Association of the Directors of Campus Ministry for twenty years of service in that organization. In 1982, I was in Boston for the annual meeting of the diocesan directors when they voted to establish the organization formally.

I have spent a lot of my years in the desert. It sounds crazy when I tell people that I love the desert, since I was born and raised on an island close to the water. But the desert grows on you. I love the cactus and the heat of the desert. One of my passions is to travel. I love to experience other cultures. I have been fortunate to travel extensively, especially when I was on my sabbaticals. I traveled in the States, Europe, Australia, New Zealand, Indonesia and Singapore. As long as my health permits, I hope I will continue to travel.

I love sports. My favorite sport is soccer. Even in the States, I still follow the Italian and the English Premiere Leagues. Whichever university I served, I took the time to attend all kinds of sports events— football, basketball (men and women), baseball, softball, volleyball, and tennis. I was asked by the football coaches to celebrate Mass for the team before their home games. I also follow professional football and baseball. My favorite teams are the San Francisco 49ers and the San Francisco Giants. I am proud to say that in my office, I have an autographed picture of my favorite player, Jerry Rice, wide receiver for the 49ers.

This introduction will not be complete if I do not include what I have learned during these forty four years of campus ministry. First of all, I have come to love working with the students. They are a great asset to the church—they are the church of today and the church of tomorrow. Without the involvement of the students, a Newman Center is dead. As a director, I have learned to empower the students so that they can learn how to use their time, talent, and treasure for building up the church on campus. Yes, students make mistakes and they stumble, but as a campus minister, I have learned to help them to learn from their mistakes. I have learned how to journey with the students. Students are very creative. I let them use their creativity. As a campus minister, I have learned to encourage the students to be the voice of the Newman Center. I have a lot of respect for the students who are involved in a Newman Center's activities, recognizing how busy students are today, often carrying a full load of credits while working to make money in order to attend the university.

I believe in the importance of inviting university staff, faculty, and administration to be visible at a Newman Center. I encourage them to be active at the Center. Students are impressed when they see their professors attending Mass on a weekend or during the week. Their presence speaks a thousand words. For a campus minister, it is valuable to get to know the administration, especially the university or college president.

Throughout the following pages, as I relate the history of campus ministry, I have inserted my own experiences of the various Newman Centers where I served. In those pages, I mention a lot of things that I learned as a campus minister. One thing is certain: Even if a program or a project works at one campus, it will not necessarily work on another. Each campus has its own identity.

I hope that you will enjoy reading this abridged history of campus ministry in the United States. As you read it, I hope that you will have a deep appreciation for our pioneers who struggled to make a dream a reality.

An Abridged History of Catholic Campus Ministry

THE CALL TO BE A CAMPUS MINISTER

It was mid-November 1962 when I was Associate Pastor at St. Mary Magdalen in Berkeley, California, that I received a phone call from then Provincial Fr. Joseph Agius, O.P. He told me of my new assignment to St. Dominic's Parish in Los Angeles, California, where I would be Associate Pastor and also part-time Newman chaplain at Occidental College, a small liberal arts college. I had been in Berkeley only a few months, so I asked the provincial to allow me to stay longer, but it was to no avail. I still remember those commanding words of Fr. Agius: "You are to report to St. Dominic on December 8." I had no clue what a Newman chaplain was! So I asked him, "What is a Newman Club (as they were commonly known then)?" He replied with his usual answer, "Son, you will learn." Since the Paulist Fathers staffed the Newman Center at the University of California, Berkeley, I went to speak to one of them. This priest was kind enough to spend some time with me in order to give me an introduction to the Newman Movement. Thus, on December 8, 1962, my campus ministry career began at Occidental College, and after forty-four years as a campus minister, I can now say that I have learned what it means to be a campus minister.

When I went to St. Dominic, I looked up Fr. George Cranham, who was the Director of Campus Ministry for the Archdiocese of Los Angeles and campus minister at Los Angeles City College. He and I met for a few weeks on a regular basis. Although there was very little literature about the ministry itself, he was instrumental in introducing me to this new ministry. Since then I have been interested in the historical development of the movement. Years ago I read Fr. John Whitney Evans' book *The Newman Movement*. This book inspired me to write an abridged history of the movement with the hope that campus ministers will take the time to read it and have an appreciation for our roots. I am also including my own experiences of campus ministry from the various sites I served.

THE BEGINNINGS—1883 TO 1907

The "Newman Movement" started as a reaction to anti-Catholicism. The movement's aim from the very beginning was to educate the students attending state colleges and universities in their faith and to take care of their spiritual needs. Established as Newman Clubs, they started to organize on various campuses, a move opposed by most U.S. bishops and Catholic colleges. Yet in spite of the struggle and lack of support from the U.S. hierarchy, the Newman Movement, known now as Catholic Campus Ministry, has grown and survived for more than a century. In fact one can say that campus ministry is alive in several state university and college campuses and even in Catholic institutions of higher learning.

The movement was born on Thanksgiving Day 1883. The Melvin Club—the predecessor of the Newman Club—was founded on that day at the University of Wisconsin, Madison. Every Thanksgiving, Mr. and Mrs. John C. Melvin hosted Catholic university students at their spacious house just across the street from the University of Wisconsin. One of those present, John J. McAnaw, a pre-law student from Ohio, accused William F. Allen, who taught ancient languages and history, of slandering the Catholic Church. Mrs. Melvin suggested if the students wanted to defend their Catholic faith and their heritage they had to learn it first. She encouraged those present to form a society for the study of Irish and Catholic history and literature. Before the day was over, a new society was born, with John J. McAnaw as its president. Timothy Harrington, one of its members, described the club as the center for much of the social life of Catholic students and source of most of the intellectual food on Catholic subjects. One should note that it was the interest of a lay student that got the Melvin Club started with the support of a dynamic Catholic laywoman who gave it its impetus.

For the next fifteen years, the club earned a reputation as "one of the most prosperous" clubs on campus. The club was open to all university students, including non-Catholics. The purpose of the club was to help Catholics attending the state university to stay in touch with their religious heritage. In addition to attending Mass and fulfilling their religious obligations, various Catholic topics were discussed during their weekly meetings.

tennis. I was asked by the football coaches to celebrate Mass for the team before their home games. I also follow professional football and baseball. My favorite teams are the San Francisco 49ers and the San Francisco Giants. I am proud to say that in my office, I have an autographed picture of my favorite player, Jerry Rice, wide receiver for the 49ers.

This introduction will not be complete if I do not include what I have learned during these forty four years of campus ministry. First of all, I have come to love working with the students. They are a great asset to the church—they are the church of today and the church of tomorrow. Without the involvement of the students, a Newman Center is dead. As a director, I have learned to empower the students so that they can learn how to use their time, talent, and treasure for building up the church on campus. Yes, students make mistakes and they stumble, but as a campus minister, I have learned to help them to learn from their mistakes. I have learned how to journey with the students. Students are very creative. I let them use their creativity. As a campus minister, I have learned to encourage the students to be the voice of the Newman Center. I have a lot of respect for the students who are involved in a Newman Center's activities, recognizing how busy students are today, often carrying a full load of credits while working to make money in order to attend the university.

I believe in the importance of inviting university staff, faculty, and administration to be visible at a Newman Center. I encourage them to be active at the Center. Students are impressed when they see their professors attending Mass on a weekend or during the week. Their presence speaks a thousand words. For a campus minister, it is valuable to get to know the administration, especially the university or college president.

Throughout the following pages, as I relate the history of campus ministry, I have inserted my own experiences of the various Newman Centers where I served. In those pages, I mention a lot of things that I learned as a campus minister. One thing is certain: Even if a program or a project works at one campus, it will not necessarily work on another. Each campus has its own identity.

I hope that you will enjoy reading this abridged history of campus ministry in the United States. As you read it, I hope that you will have a deep appreciation for our pioneers who struggled to make a dream a reality.

Almost ten years after that Thanksgiving Day, Harrington took his experience of the Melvin Club to the University of Pennsylvania, where he was studying medicine. Seeing the need for a similar club on Penn's campus, he founded the Newman Club in 1893. After the Christmas holidays of 1892, Harrington suggested creating a Catholic club modeled after the Melvin Club to a few Catholic students who attended St. James Church in Philadelphia. In the autumn of 1893, Harrington met with about twenty fellow students to form the Newman Club, the first of many to be founded later. They met with St. James' pastor, Fr. P. J. Garvey, and the club got off the ground. Harrington, the club's first president, recalled nearly thirty years later that "no better name could be found" for this organization of young Catholics on a university "than the name of the great English Cardinal" John Henry Newman, convert to Catholicism, scholar, and founder of the Oxford Movement in England.[1] One might note that Cardinal Newman was beatified by Pope Benedict XVI in Birmingham, England on September 19, 2011. According to Harrington, the aim of the Catholic club "would give the Catholics of this university a chance to come together, to know one another, to discuss subjects of interest to Catholic students, and possibly to increase somewhat the opportunities for social life among strangers coming to Philadelphia."[2]

The pioneers who began Newman Clubs recognized that the growing number of Catholics attending state colleges and universities desired support and instruction in their faith. Most of these students had no other choice, since Catholic education was expensive and unaffordable for the majority of Catholics. A Catholic club on a state university campus would give support to these students in the practice and the knowledge of their faith.

The founders had a dream. Inspired by the "Newman Idea"— Cardinal Newman's vision of establishing a center for Catholic pastoral and intellectual life to preserve the faith and morals of young Catholics attending Oxford University in England—the early Newman chaplains wanted to establish schools of religion next to state colleges and universities, which were increasingly becoming more secular.

As student enrollment in public institutions of higher education was swelling—in 1900, 280,000 students were enrolled; by 1920 that

---

1   Timothy L. Harrington, M.D., "Memories of the Early Days of the Oldest Newman Club," *Newman Quarterly*, Summer 1921.
2   Ibid.

number had doubled; and two decades later, enrollment was up to 1.5 million—so was the number of Catholics attending state colleges and universities. Most of the U.S. bishops did not approve of this trend. The Catholic students who attended public institutions in the early 1900s were condemned by pastors and bishops, who said the students were exposing their faith and morals to corruption while seeking worldly advancement. In 1906, John Murphy Cardinal Farley, Archbishop of New York, charged these students with perpetrating "an act of unpardonable disloyalty and grossest ingratitude" to God Himself. Meanwhile, Archbishop Patrick William Riordan of San Francisco insisted that if the Church neglected the Catholic young men and women attending state universities, many educated laypersons would be lost.

In response to the spiritual needs of Catholics attending state universities and colleges, in 1888 Catholic clubs started to emerge. That year, Catholic students at Cornell University organized the Cornell Catholic Union, one of the first organized Catholic groups at a secular university. In the early 1900s, it was renamed the Newman Club. Similar groups were established at the University of Michigan in 1889 as Catholic students joined together to form the Guild of Catholic students, named after John Henry Cardinal Newman, at Brown University in 1892 and Harvard in 1893.

By 1905, besides the aforementioned Catholic clubs on campuses, Catholic student clubs or societies were organized on other campuses, among them the University of California, Berkeley (1898); University of Iowa (1901); Columbia University (1902); University of Chicago (1902); University of Minnesota (1903); and University of Missouri (1903). The purpose of these clubs was to help students learn, defend, and spread their Catholic faith and to offer mutual support to one another. Social events such as dances, smokers, teas, and sports activities were scheduled in order to attract members, especially freshmen. These clubs adopted a variety of names, such as DeSmedt Club in Idaho, Foley Guild in Michigan, the Catholic Club at Harvard, Spaulding Guild at the University of Illinois, Louis Pasteur Club at Tufts University, and St. Melania's Club at Wellesley College. The University of California, Berkeley, and the University of Texas used the name Newman. Since the majority of the clubs did not have their own facilities, the students met wherever they could, including in Knights of Columbus halls, church basements, YMCA buildings, private homes, and university classrooms. University presidents seldom denied permission to use university property, acknowledging the moral influence that these religious clubs provided. These clubs flourished when they had a very good spiritual adviser, such as in the case of the Spaulding Guild at the University of Illinois, led by Fr. John H. Cannon from 1905–1911.

FULL-TIME APPOINTMENTS

At the University of Wisconsin in Madison, three hundred Catholic students signed a petition asking Archbishop Sebastian Messmer to authorize the organization of a Catholic student association, to appoint a chaplain, and to build a chapel close to the university. Their desire for pastoral care was welcomed, and on September 17, 1906, Fr. Henry C. Hengell was appointed the first full-time Newman chaplain of the newly formed Catholic Students Association, which was the successor of the Melvin Club. Three other dioceses followed: the Archdiocese of San Francisco, which appointed a full-time chaplain at the University of California, Berkeley; the Diocese of Rochester, New York, at Cornell University; and the Diocese of Austin at the University of Texas, Austin.

Because this new phenomenon of appointing full-time chaplains at state universities was taking place, in 1906 Fr. John J. Farrell of Harvard formed the first chaplains' organization, called the American Federation of Spiritual Directors of College Catholic Clubs. Chaplains from New England, Georgia, the Midwest, California, and Canada joined the federation. This federation, a support group for Newman chaplains, lasted for a few years.

After the start of the 1906–07 academic year, the Milwaukee archdiocesan newspaper, *The Catholic Citizen*, acknowledged that the "Catholic Student Movement at universities of the country is growing wonderfully." After reporting various appointments of chaplains in different state campuses, it pointed out that "all these facts (and there are others) are significant of a wide spread movement to follow the Catholic young man to the non-Catholic university and provide for him there."[3] A 1907 survey of Catholics enrolled in institutions of higher education revealed that of fourteen thousand such students, two-thirds were on non-Catholic campuses.[4]

The Paulists and Dominicans were invited by bishops to minister to

---

3   *The Catholic Citizen* (Milwaukee), November 24, 1906.
4   Catholic Educational Association, Reports 4, 1907.

the students attending state universities. Four bishops invited the Paulist Fathers to establish university missions on four campuses, while six other bishops appointed chaplains to minister at Newman Clubs. Bishop N. A. Gallagher of Galveston invited the Paulist Fathers to begin their ministry at the University of Texas, Austin, in 1908. They built St. Austin's Church, which was completed in December 1908. In August of that same year, the Dominicans of the Western Province were invited by Bishop Edward J. O'Dea of Seattle to establish a parish at the growing university district in Seattle to take care of the spiritual needs of the University of Washington students. Fr. F. D. Driscoll, O.P., started the parish and the Newman Center.

The growth and the chaplains' hard work were becoming evident over the next ten to fifteen years as new developments took place. On May 2, 1909, the cornerstone for St. Paul's Chapel at the University of Wisconsin, Madison, was laid; the chapel was dedicated on January 27, 1910. St. Austin and St. Paul were the first two chapels built at American secular universities. With the financial support of Archbishop Riordan of San Francisco, Newman Hall was built in 1910, serving the University of California, Berkeley. On the University of Texas campus in Austin, a 21-room center—with social rooms, offices, a library, a lecture hall, and quarters for the chaplains—opened for the Newman Club in 1914. Four years later, a four-story women's dormitory opened, administered by the Dominican Sisters of Galveston. The Newman Club at the University of Texas was the first to develop a liturgical educational program. At the University of Illinois, Champaign, Father John A. O'Brien, who was already teaching accredited courses in religion, was taking the first steps to build a complex of buildings that included a large chapel, a recreation hall, a library, classrooms, a kitchen, and a dining hall adequate for feeding the six hundred men and women who would live in the two-story dormitory wings sponsored by the Newman Club. Although the bishops gave some financial support toward these projects, the chaplains and alumni were mainly responsible for fund raising.

TENSIONS AROSE

As the Newman Movement was taking hold on state campuses, tensions arose between those who supported Newman halls at public universities and those who feared that, by doing so, Catholic students would not attend Catholic institutions, as they believed was best. Bishops, clergy, and laity could be found on both sides of the argument. Bishops and Catholic educators were divided over the interpretation of Pope Pius X's encyclical letter *Acerbo Nimis*, published April 15, 1905, which is considered the papal charter of the Newman Movement. The pope wrote, "In the larger cities, and especially where universities, colleges and secondary schools are located, let classes in religion be organized to instruct in the truths of faith and in the practice of Christian life the youths who attend the public schools from which all religious teaching is banned."[5] Some insisted that the Pope meant to have organized classes about the faith on secular campuses, while others maintained that the Pope was ordering the erection of permanent buildings for the study of Catholic doctrine and morals.

Aware of this tension, Fr. Hengell, chaplain at the Newman Club at the University of Wisconsin, Madison, wrote in 1914: "Even the clergy were often either hostile or indifferent to the project (referring to his building a chapel) because, from a theoretical standpoint, they conceived the chapel to be a move in competition with Catholic colleges and universities instead of a practical effort to meet the actual conditions at the universities where hundreds of Catholic students are starved out of their religious faith by a lack of food to feed it."[6]

NATIONAL ORGANIZATION

As more students were attending state universities and colleges, there was a felt need to establish an association for Catholic students in order to have more cooperation among the various Catholic clubs. Such an attempt to form a student federation failed in 1903, but by 1907, stronger leadership among Catholic students had emerged. Thus, the Catholic Student Association of America (CSAA) was established in April 1908 at Purdue University in Indiana. Raymond V. Achatz was elected president. This association lasted until 1915.

Representatives from fifteen state universities (ten Midwestern, four Ivy League, and one West Coast) agreed on six purposes for the new national association:

---

5   Pope Pius X, *Acerbo Nimis* (Rome, 15 April 1905), no. 23.

6   Bill Kasdorf and Phil Haslanger, *Aggiornamento: St. Paul's University Chapel* (Madison, WI: The University Catholic Center, 1974), 3.

1. To bring Catholic students of America into closer relationship with one another through their local organization;
2. To effect the establishment of local organizations at non-Catholic universities and colleges where they do not exist;
3. To make a concentrated effort to secure special spiritual direction from the clergy;
4. To further the good will already existing between Catholics and non-Catholics;
5. To endeavor to correct occasional misconception of Catholicism; and
6. To promote among the members unswerving loyalty to the Catholic faith.

They also sought out a bishop to serve as the "national spiritual director" who would be elected for life. CSAA published a journal titled *The Catholic Student* at irregular intervals between 1909 and 1916.

When bishops became more interested in the Catholic students attending public universities, they began to prescribe the qualifications and tasks for the chaplains. On March 13, 1911, Archbishop Riordan of San Francisco, in a letter addressed to Rev. John J. Hughes, C.S.P., outlined the requirements of a university chaplain. He wrote:

> The requirements of the Newman Hall are, as you know, somewhat peculiar. Not everyone would be at home in a university atmosphere, or be successful with the students. He must have a natural sympathy with intellectual pursuits, at the same time possess the qualifications which will enable him to interest and hold the students of whom he is in charge. There is required besides a patience and a perseverance exercised mainly in the work of personal contact with the individual student.[7]

Another step in the right direction took place when the Federation of College Catholic Clubs (FCCC) of Greater New York was established on October 28, 1915, by Sr. Mary F. Higgins, a member of the Society of the Daughters of the Heart of Mary. She taught education at Hunter College in New York and was the adviser to the Catholic students' society, the Barat Club. Their hope was to expand it to a national organization,

---

7 Archbishop Patrick William Riordan to John Hughes, 13 March 1911, Archdiocese of San Francisco, Archives.

which they did, and the federation soon replaced CSAA. John Murphy Cardinal Farley of New York agreed to serve as its Episcopal patron; John Michael Kieran, Dean of Hunter College, was elected its first president; and Fr. John W. Keogh, chaplain at the University of Pennsylvania known as "Mr. Newman," was appointed its chaplain. The club members were encouraged to adopt the name of John Henry Cardinal Newman.

The new federation held its first gathering at Cliff Haven, New York, in the summer of 1916. Fifty student delegates and adult advisers from New York, Massachusetts, New Jersey, and Pennsylvania shared classes and prayer along with hiking, swimming, and boating at the Catholic summer school. This federation gave the basic shape to the Newman Movement for the next half-century. The federation members agreed to the following principles for the new national association, which were very similar to the goals set by the very first student association (the CSAA):

1. To form local clubs for students' support;
2. To make clubs part of the federation to secure the highest possible development and efficiency while respecting their independence;
3. To establish provinces to carry on the national program according to the needs of the region;
4. To obtain approval of the local bishop in order for the local club to be a member;
5. To pledge loyalty to the teaching and the authority of the Church;
6. To establish the *Newman Quarterly*; and
7. To establish the office of chaplain general.

The new federation decided to invite all similar Catholic groups to affiliate with FCCC, hoping that through cooperation and an exchange of ideas, the movement would prosper and expand to include all the non-Catholic colleges and universities in the United States. By 1919, five provinces were set up with headquarters in Philadelphia, New York, Boston, Pittsburgh, and Albany.

In 1917, the first issue of the *Newman Quarterly* was published with Dr. Alexis Coleman, Professor of English at City College of New York, serving as the editor. This publication was replaced by the *Newman News* in 1926. The monthly *Newman News* provided the clubs with articles and items more attuned to the immediate needs of the students. In 1949, *Newman News* was replaced by *Newman News Notes*. During the 50s and the early 60s, many Newman Clubs established their own publications, a practice that is still common today.

NEWMAN AND RELATIONS WITH HIERARCHY

In 1920, Arthur Monahan, head of the Bureau of Education at the National Catholic Welfare Council (predecessor to today's United States Conference of Catholic Bishops and hereafter referred to as NCWC), showed great interest in Catholic students attending secular colleges and universities, after his bureau sponsored a survey that revealed that forty thousand Catholics attended state colleges and universities compared to nineteen thousand enrolled in Catholic colleges. The following year, the NCWC Administrative Committee unanimously supported the work of the Newman Clubs all over the country. The Bureau of Education helped promote Newman Clubs by issuing three thousand brochures explaining the role of Newman Clubs, especially the service they provided in grounding every student attending state university and college in Catholic principles. In 1922, the Bureau of Education stated that Newman Clubs were "one of the most powerful aids" in developing Catholic leaders for all branches of Catholic education.[8]

Although the Bureau of Education was convinced of the importance of the presence of Newman Clubs on state universities, the bishops still maintained that Catholics should attend Catholic colleges and universities. Constant tension between the Newman Movement and the U.S. bishops and religious orders running Catholic colleges and universities continued, fueled by the fear that if the bishops approved the movement, Catholic higher education might not survive.

To promote Catholic education, the U.S. bishops established "Catholic College Week" in January 1922; the week was held from April 30 to May 6 of that year. Seven daily ads were placed in Catholic publications with two goals: first, to promote Catholic college education, and second, to convince parents of the advantages of Catholic colleges. Catholic colleges and universities were urged to schedule a "Catholic College Day" on their campus.

But in the midst of the struggle, there was always a glimmer of hope. In May 1922, much to the delight of the Newman chaplains and clubs, Pope Pius XI congratulated the Newman Federation for the "good works"

---

8 John Whitney Evans, *The Newman Movement: Roman Catholics in American Higher Education 1883-1971* (Notre Dame Press, 1980), 20.

they were doing "for the Catholic youth at the various Newman halls situated near large secular universities."[9]

By 1923, Monahan's representative assured the FCCC that the "NCWC considers Newman Clubs as part of the Catholic Educational System."[10] In 1924, Fr. John O'Brien, chaplain at the University of Illinois, Champaign, returned from the Vatican with a special blessing, signaling the pope's approval for the educational programs of the Newman Movement. The authorities in Rome seemed to appreciate how the Newman Movement was attempting to fulfill the mandate of Pope Pius X who had recommended that "schools of religion be founded" at public universities, as was mentioned earlier.

Over the years, the relationship between Newman Clubs and NCWC was unpredictable; at one time, NCWC supported the Newman Movement, but in 1925, NCWC withdrew its support. Newman Clubs were no longer considered part of the Catholic educational system, even though NCWC had declared they were just two years prior. In fact, in May 1926, the NCWC Department of Education issued a booklet stating "the presence of a Newman Club does not warrant a Catholic parent thinking for a moment that the religious needs of his/her child will be as well cared for as in a Catholic College."[11] It warned parents to be aware of their children's religious needs, indicating those needs would better be met in a Catholic college than in a Newman Club. These statements influenced the decision of Catholic students to attend Catholic colleges and universities instead of the public ones, and so, by 1930, two-thirds of the 158,000 Catholics in higher education attended Catholic colleges and universities.

In the 1926 FCCC conference, the Newman Club chaplains met in a private session for the first time to discuss their concern that many of the clubs were becoming primarily social. After this meeting, greater emphasis was placed on Communion breakfasts and discussions about religious and moral problems. The chaplains inaugurated the Newman Club Liturgical Movement and felt that it was the movement's mission to develop spirituality among the students.

From 1926–1930, Fr. John W. Keogh, chaplain at the University of Pennsylvania, developed the concept of the "Newman Idea," known

---

9   Ibid., 72.
10 Ibid., 77.
11 Ibid., 77.

also as Newmanism. The Newman Idea included "three basic elements: one pastoral, one instructional, one related to the leadership the bishop of each diocese should provide."[12] The Newman Idea, in its basic form, forecast the present shape of the Catholic Campus Ministry Association.

With the 1928 dedication of the Newman Foundation at the University of Illinois, Champaign, and with the unqualified approval of Bishop Edward R. Dunne, Bishop of Peoria, Chaplain Fr. John O'Brien saw his 1918 dream fulfilled in just ten years. The project, subsidized by a million-dollar capital campaign, consisted of lecture halls, a library, seminar rooms, dining facilities, and dormitories for men and women. The project, known as "a Catholic college for the University of Illinois," was an amazing accomplishment considering the severe opposition from U.S. bishops; presidents of Catholic universities; Jesuit publications *America, Woodstock Letters,* and *Civilta Cattolica*; and the College and University Department of the NCEA. In his book *Adapting to America: Catholic Jesuits and Higher education in the Twentieth Century,* William P. Leahy, S.J., wrote, "Some of them (Jesuits) also joined in efforts to discredit the Newman apostolate and dissuade Catholics from attending secular schools…through their journals, Jesuits became leading critics of the Newman apostolate…printed fifteen articles in 1925 and 1926 discussing the strengths of Catholic education and the defects of the Newman Club."[13] Attacks on the Newman Movement, common in the Catholic press in the mid-1920s, diminished as Catholic fears about loss of faith in a Protestant culture lessened.

Besides building the Newman Foundation, Fr. O'Brien taught accredited courses in Catholicism at the state university following the example of pioneer Fr. Edward Murray, the first Catholic priest on record to teach courses in religion accredited by a public university (University of Iowa) in 1911.

SEEKING HIERARCHICAL RECOGNITION

"Why does a Newman Center exist?" This was the question tackled at the federation's conference held July 2–4, 1928, in Toronto. Fr. Keogh encouraged the two hundred delegates and fourteen chaplains

---

12 Ibid., 83.

13 William P. Leahy, S.J., *Adapting to America: Catholic Jesuits and Higher Education in the Twentieth Century* (Georgetown University Press, 1991), 41.

representing one hundred twenty clubs (more than seventy-five percent of the total) to give a clear answer to the question. They resolved unanimously that Newman Clubs are based upon the encyclical letter *Acerbo Nimis*, in which Pius X commanded that schools of religion be established at all secular institutions of higher learning.[14] The delegates were commissioned to take this resolution back to their respective clubs where they would emphasize the need for systematic religious instruction, similar to the 1926 focus emphasized by the chaplains.

The following year, Archbishop John T. McNicholas of Cincinnati set up a School of Religion at the city's metropolitan university. He referred to this center as the "Newman Foundation," a place for research and lectures in scripture, scholastic philosophy, and history. He tried to have the courses offered by the center accredited by the university.

In the late 1920s, Fr. Keogh, acting as the chaplain general, wanted the Newman Movement to be part of Catholic Action, defined in 1927 by Pope Pius XI as the "participation of the laity in the apostolate on the hierarchy." Fr. Keogh asserted that the Newman Movement had the same objectives as Catholic Action, namely, the development of the spiritual life of the students, sound doctrine, and working hand-in-hand with the hierarchy. At the June 1929 federation convention held in Cincinnati, the delegates approved the association with the Catholic Action movement. Catholic Action themes were chosen for the next few annual conferences, and Newman Movement leadership hoped this action would advance the acceptance of the movement by the U.S. bishops.

In 1930 Fr. Keogh recorded that about half of the seventy thousand Catholics in secular institutions belonged to one hundred sixty-four clubs, one hundred eleven of which were affiliates of the eight fully organized provinces of the federation. About thirty of these clubs had chaplains, with only ten chaplains serving on a full-time basis. In December 1937, representatives of eighteen Catholic institutions formed the National Federation of Catholic College Students (NFCCS), whose purpose was to counteract communist-inspired student clubs by making "authentic Catholic Action" a force among national and international organizations.

In the early 1930s, Fr. Wlodimir Ledóchowski, S.J., the superior general of the Society of Jesus, asked the Jesuit magazine *America* to stop attacking the Newman Movement. He did this after *America* urged

---

14 Pope Pius X, *Acerbo Nimis,* no. 23

Catholics to boycott the School of Religion at the University of Iowa, claiming that the School of Religion was a poor substitute for the kind of instruction in religion to be gained under strictly Catholic auspices. Fr. Ledóchowski refuted this claim, instead insisting that Newman Club work was also the work of the Society of Jesus.

In 1936 national chaplain Fr. Paul A. Deery of Indiana University approached Bishop Edwin V. O'Hara of Great Falls, Montana, then the chair of the NCWC National Confraternity of Christian Doctrine, suggesting the linkage of the Newman Movement with the confraternity. Bishop O'Hara, who had served as a Newman chaplain at the University of Oregon, was delighted by the proposal. So, in 1937, in order to get the Newman Movement accepted by the bishops, the movement became part of the Confraternity of Christian Doctrine, which allowed its reentry into the NCWC in 1940.

Along the way, some bishops continued to believe in the importance of Newman ministry. At the 1938 convention, to the delight of the delegates, Cincinnati Archbishop McNicholas offered a challenge to his fellow bishops: "Assuming that Catholic students attending secular colleges and universities in the United States today number one hundred thousand, we have one hundred thousand reasons to care for their spiritual well being."[15] Some Newman leaders regarded this challenge as a turning point in the acceptance of the Newman Movement.

In order to band together those persons who had been prominent in Newman Club work, the John Henry Cardinal Newman Honorary Society was formed in 1938 with the following objectives:

1. To further the Newman Club program;
2. To honor Catholic students, alumni, and chaplains who have aided the Church through the Newman Club Movement; and
3. To bring greater honor to the name of John Henry Cardinal Newman.

In 1949 the Society decided to give an annual John Henry Newman award to an outstanding Catholic lay person involved in the Church and the Newman Apostolate at local, regional, and national levels. Among the recipients were Clare Booth Luce and Mr. and Mrs. Frank Sheed.

---

15 Evans, *The Newman Movement*, 91.

WORLD WAR II AND THE INTERNATIONAL MOVEMENT OF CATHOLIC STUDENTS

Student leaders of the NFCCS, Phi Kappa Theta (a fraternity of Catholic men), and the Newman Movement organized the 1939 World Congress of the International Movement of Catholic Students (IMCS) at Fordham University and other Catholic universities. Right in the middle of the congress, Germany invaded Poland, and World War II started. Hundreds of European students were stranded in the United States. What was to be done?

The first step was for all representatives from the countries at war to pray, eat, and work together in order to be witnesses for peace. Second, they needed to convince Francis Joseph Cardinal Spellman of New York to help them find temporary shelter for the students who were stranded at the end of the congress; as a result, scholarships, jobs, and permanent housing were located. Third, they decided to establish a secretariat to help administer IMCS for the duration of the war, because the IMCS international headquarters were isolated in Switzerland. These objectives were accomplished through the sacrifice, commitment, and collaboration of students and chaplains.

NEWMAN MOVEMENT RECOGNITION

As the Newman Movement was struggling to find its place in the structure of the Church, the following suggestion was made: "Why not bring the Newman Federation and the NFCCS together as a section of the proposed Youth Department?"[16] In July 1940 at Niagara University, the bishops' National Catholic Youth Committee devised a plan to unite the two entities into the College and University Section of the NCWC Youth Department. This announcement was very well received by the Newman leadership, because it gave national recognition to the Newman Movement. The national chaplain, Fr. Donald M. Cleary of Cornell University, remarked that after many years, the federation's status as a stepchild was over. The new section was coordinated under the Catholic Action movement, fulfilling the vision of the popes at that time. A new constitution, drastically different from the 1938 one, was drafted by Bishop John A. Duffy, Bishop of Buffalo, and Fr. Vincent Mooney C.S.C.,

---

16 Evans, *The Newman Movement*, 95.

head of the Catholic Youth Bureau in the NCWC. It was adopted in June 1942.

Influenced by the philosophy of Catholic Action, under the new constitution the federation was to assist when invited by the local ordinary; previously, the federation existed to organize Catholic students. Furthermore, the national chaplain was to be appointed by the Episcopal moderator instead of being elected to serve as spiritual advisor. Again, all policies were to be reviewed by the Episcopal moderator, the supreme authority of the organization, in contrast to the previous one in which all policies were executed by the executive committee and approved by delegates at their annual meeting.

A manual for Newman leaders, compiled by Fr. Cleary, was published by the Youth Department of the NCWC in May 1942. The purpose of this small booklet, published after consultation with "hundreds of chaplains and Newman Club members" was "to provide Newman Club chaplains and officers with a guidebook to enable them to form Newman Clubs where none exists and to strengthen those already in existence."[17]

This manual included the history of the Newman Federation; gave some guidelines about the functions of chaplains and students; provided a model club constitution and by-laws; included tips for starting a Newman Club; listed works in which members might want to get involved; and proposed establishing religion courses at secular institutions. The manual was to be sent to all of the clubs that were sponsored and authorized by the bishops. Although this manual was addressed to Newman Clubs, the preface encouraged students to enroll at Catholic institutions even while simultaneously recognizing the fact "that over one hundred and fifty thousand Catholic students are not in Catholic colleges but are in secular institutions" for reasons of finance and geography.[18]

By the end of 1941, with the rapid growth of the Newman Movement, more geographic provinces were formed, covering all of the United States, Canada, Hawaii, and Puerto Rico. The purpose of these provinces was "to carry out the program of the federation and to unify the forces of the clubs in their respective regions."[19] The chairperson of each province was a member of the federation's executive committee,

---

17 Rev. Donald L. Cleary, ed., *Newman Club Federation: A Handbook for Chaplains and Officers of Newman Foundations and Clubs* (The Newman Club Federation, 1942), 3

18 Ibid., 3.

19 Ibid., 14.

which was the governing body. The establishment of a central office in Washington was a great help to the federation, to the provinces, and to all the clubs.

POST-WORLD WAR II AND THE GI BILL

After the Second World War, the texture of American Catholicism changed dramatically. Immigrant Catholics or their children had become sufficiently prosperous to aspire for a better life in the suburbs and for higher education. Due to the G.I. Bill of Rights signed on June 22, 1944, by President Franklin D. Roosevelt, the impact on the Catholic community was permanent. Catholics from all ethnic backgrounds, who otherwise would not have had the opportunity to pursue college education, were able to enroll in state colleges and universities. Catholics became more assimilated into American culture.

Fr. Clyde Crews, in his book *American and Catholic*, stated that "hundreds of thousands of Catholic veterans soon found themselves on state university campuses, far from the 'Catholic Ghetto', exposed to a vast pluralism of faith and ideas."[20] Because of this increase, new Newman Centers and Clubs emerged across the country, and it was estimated that six hundred Newman Clubs in the United States, Canada, Puerto Rico, Hawaii, Philippine Islands, Australia, and China were active. Bishop Leo Pursley of Fort Wayne, Indiana, remarked, "All of a sudden the large number of Catholics going to secular colleges stood up and hit us between the eyes."[21]

In 1947 the New York province issued "The Responsible Catholic Program," which was nationally adopted three years later. This program attempted to form mature, prayerful, and socially conscientious Catholic graduates attending state colleges and universities. The federation set up an external affairs department in 1947 to provide representation in various national and international organizations of both secular and religious natures. It also organized the "Newman mission" with the purpose of helping to recruit volunteers for foreign and home missions.

The effort for the missions underscores the fact that social justice was a key component in the history of campus ministry and still is

---

20 Clyde F. Crews, *America and Catholic: A Popular history of Catholicism in the United States*, rev. ed. (Cincinnati, OH: St. Anthony Messenger press, 2004), 135.
21 Evans, *The Newman Movement*, 99.

today as outlined in the fourth aspect—educating for justice—of the U.S. bishops' 1985 pastoral letter on campus ministry, "Empowered by the Spirit." From the 1948 conventions on, the federation consistently opposed all campus discrimination based on race. In fact the Southeastern province did not hold its convention in 1956 because the host university wanted the housing arrangements to be segregated by color. Furthermore, because of its interest in the welfare of the growing number of foreign students attending American colleges and universities, the federation set up an Aid to Foreign Students Committee in 1949.

Starting in the 1950s and continuing for several years, Newman Clubs established rituals for admitting members to the clubs. The 1942 handbook had already suggested that every club should have an initiation ceremony for its new members. The members were encouraged to receive the sacraments frequently, participate in the annual retreats and mission, make First Friday devotions, pray the rosary daily, and make the Stations of the Cross during Lent. They developed choirs that sang at Sunday High Masses. Liturgically, Newman Clubs were ahead of their time—dialogue homilies, singing hymns, and offertory processions were part of their life. Additionally, several vocations to the priesthood and religious life emerged from these clubs. An official from the University of Notre Dame who attended the 1950 Newman Federation conference commented that Newman Clubs' Catholic members attending secular institutions were so much more apostolic in their zeal than students on Catholic campuses.

EDUCATIONAL OPPORTUNITIES

At the mid-century convention in Cleveland, Ohio, in June 1950, one thousand delegates, eight chaplains, and three bishops gathered for a gala celebration of the Newman Movement, which had survived more than sixty years of struggle and rejection, both on campus and within the Church. An important question was raised: Could the Newman Movement provide educational possibilities and theological literacy for its members?

At this convention, the clergy announced the formation of the National Newman Chaplains' Association. Fr. Edward Duncan, the Newman chaplain at the University of Illinois, Champaign, who served as the national chaplain to the student federation, was appointed the association's first president, and an advisory board to the president was established. The purpose of this new association was to "further the work of the chaplains on a local and national level, to pool their spiritual, intellectual and organizational resources, and to use the zeal and talents of all the chaplains in perfecting the Newman apostolate."[22] From 1969 onward, this association became known as the Catholic Campus Ministry Association (CCMA).

In response to the question raised at the convention about educational opportunities for student leaders, federation leaders launched educational summer seminars for the students. The first seminar was sponsored by the University of Notre Dame and the Ohio Valley Province in 1952. The twenty-six students who attended were offered a week-long series of lectures and workshops on theology, liturgy, the laity and the church, and ecumenical relations.

CLERICALISM VS. STUDENT LEADERSHIP

In July 1952, Fr. Thomas A. Carlin, O.S.F.S., was the first priest appointed to serve as the first full-time executive secretary of the Newman Club Federation. This appointment was well received by the chaplains, but the students were afraid that the clerics were taking over. Prior to this appointment, all executive secretaries appointed since 1941 (when this office started) had been lay persons.

The secretary's title changed several times over the years. In 1955, the secretary was known as Coordinating Secretary of the National Newman Club Federation; in 1962, it was changed to Coordinating Secretary of the National Newman Apostolate; in 1966, the person in this position was called Director of the National Newman Apostolate; in 1969, the title changed once again to Director of Campus Ministry Division and moved from the Youth Department to the Department of Education at the U.S. Catholic Conference of Bishops; and today, this position is known as the Assistant Secretary for Higher Education and Campus Ministry.

As previously stated, there was disagreement regarding leadership in the 1950s. Students believed there was too much clerical bureaucracy in the running of the federation, now that a priest was the executive secretary of the federation. At the meeting that took place at the University of Colorado in June 1953, Msgr. Robert Tracy of Louisiana

---

22 Ibid., 183.

State University issued a statement known as "The Boulder Memo." In this memo, he wrote that the local chaplain should moderate and not run the Newman Club. He emphasized the importance of student initiatives both locally and nationally. His memo recognized the tension that existed between clerical and student leadership at the national level, and he suggested establishing clear, agreed-upon lines of authority that left great room for student initiatives. Fr. Paul J. Hallinan of the Cleveland Intercollegiate Newman Club pointed out that students brought innovation to the Newman Movement while the chaplains contributed stability.

In May 1955, the chaplains' association issued a statement titled "Principles and Policies of the Newman Club Movement." While admitting that the best place for Catholic students was at a Catholic college, the statement pointed out that the Newman Apostolate was the response to three hundred thousand Catholic young men and women who were enrolled in secular campuses. Furthermore, the statement encouraged more cooperation between Catholic and non-Catholic centers of culture, more trained priests for the Newman Movement, more attractive and effective centers, and more cooperation from the entire Catholic intellectual effort at the college and university level. The statement concluded with Bishop Maurice Schexnayder's words: "We must not do as little as we can for the Catholic student in the secular college and university, but as much as we can."[23]

This statement helped the chaplains to earn a place within the College and University Section of the National Catholic Educational Association in 1955. At the convention that year, the federation created a Religious Education Committee to promote Catholicism's rich cultural heritage and to contribute to the development of the Catholic intellectual tradition in the United States. Delegates believed that "a good Catholic is an informed Catholic" and urged local centers to establish libraries and to form local boards of education so that they could implement educational programs for the students. Recognizing the importance of religious literacy, the local chaplains set up educational programs in their respective centers.

Squabbles took place between the chaplains' association and the NCWC Youth Department with regard to the role of the executive secretary of the Newman Club Federation in the department. Both

---

23 Ibid., 119.

Bishop Schexnayder, a former Newman chaplain and Episcopal moderator of the Newman Federation from 1952 to 1960, and Msgr. Howard Carroll, the NCWC executive secretary, intervened. Paulist Fr. Charles Albright who served at Wayne State University was named the coordinating secretary of the National Newman Club Federation at the NCWC Youth Department in July 1955, which was a boost to the Newman Movement.

FINANCIAL COMMITMENT

In 1957 the chaplains' association resolved that the future of the Newman Movement depended largely upon the establishment of a stable financial arrangement. For many years, the federation's financial support came from the dues paid by the students and chaplains' assessment. Therefore, the association wanted to explore the idea of setting up a national incorporated and tax-exempt foundation, and Msgr. James E. Rea, chaplain at Columbia University, served as president of the temporary board set up by the foundation.

The financial situation of the Newman Movement benefitted from the fact that eleven priests who had served as Newman chaplains became bishops in the 1950s. This reality advanced the cause of the Newman Movement as these bishops kept the problems of the movement in front of the hierarchy. These bishops also promoted the appointments of more chaplains, encouraged the building of Newman Centers, and forged closer links between the federation and the bishops. As an example, in 1956, Bishop Schexnayder was able to obtain a $5,000 yearly subsidy from Our Sunday Visitor Press in Huntington, Indiana, to finance the Newman Federation's educational material. Even though the hierarchy had refused to finance the project, this bishop helped to secure the necessary funding for the project. Two years later, Schexnayder was able to get the bishops to agree that the Newman Federation was its official agency in secular higher education.

In order to help the present student and chaplain organizations, the Newman Alumni Club Association was established at the 1957 national convention held in New York City. A similar alumni association had been formed in 1924, but it lasted only a few years. It was understood from the beginning that the association would not stifle student leadership by holding office that properly belonged to students, so they outlined their twofold purpose:

1. To encourage the formation and development of Newman Alumni clubs with the goal of fostering the development of the Newman Movement; and
2. To join these clubs with the national alumni association for mutual benefit and cooperative action.

NEWMAN AND EDUCATION

Not surprisingly, education has been another key component in campus ministry. In 1958 five Newman Schools of Catholic Thought were established, resulting in instruction for five hundred students at Newman Clubs. These numbers doubled within two years. Twenty-six provinces set up weekend "capsule schools," and chaplains and students alike hailed these seminars as the "most valuable" educational experience the federation provided.[24] During this period, some wealthier Newman Centers engaged speakers for a quarter or a semester as "theologians-in-residence." Even today, some Newman Centers have a theologian-in-residence, such as at the University of Toledo in Ohio; the University of Iowa; and the University of Illinois, Chicago. The national office provided good educational material that was received enthusiastically by both students and chaplains. Chaplains experimented in various ways to design courses according to the needs and resources of their own campuses. In spite of the difficulties that the federation was facing on the national level, it was growing on the diocesan level.

During the academic year of 1958–59, fifty new Catholic student centers were under construction. Four Schools of Catholic Thought were sponsored by the movement, along with eight area seminars and twenty-one leadership weekends. Additionally, a conference for club presidents was held in the interest of developing Catholic cultural and theological leadership.

In 1959, the leaders of the Newman Movement published a leaflet titled "The Battle of the Twentieth Century Will Be Fought for the Minds of the Youth." The leaders questioned the wisdom of the Church's policy that limited their ministry to social and pastoral matters. Since the campuses were the nation's centers for intellectual development,

---

24 Ibid., 114.

the chaplains felt the need to fulfill their original commitment—the instruction of the students in the truths of the faith and in the principles of Christian life.

The growth of the movement was visibly seen in the growth of the national Newman Chaplains Association. This association, which started with eight charter members in 1950, counted among its members more than half of the estimated five hundred priests assigned to Newman Clubs just ten years later. Thirty-one priests chaired various committees such as new chaplains' training, education, international students, liturgy and music, building and planning, and policy and agenda.

Ironically, an editorial titled "Catholic Values on the Secular" that appeared in the May 21, 1960, issue of *America* stated, "While the perennial argument for and against Catholic undergraduates attending non-Catholic universities and colleges have been bandied back and forth, a new factor has entered the debate—simple necessity." The editorial suggested founding "a new kind of Newman Club more to the scale of 'Catholic Institute,' complete with a library, lounge, study facilities, lecture halls, seminar rooms and above all a faculty component to create a scholarly climate of Christian culture that attracts and challenges students" to handle the educational needs of college-bound Catholics; the Church simply could not educate them all in Catholic institutions.

Also appearing in *America* that week was an article by Paulist seminarian George R. Fitzgerald, titled "Catholics in Secular Colleges." This article endorsed the need for Newman Clubs on secular campuses. Fitzgerald's article generated a heavy flow of letters to the editor, revealing the wide range of views held by Catholics on this complex issue; these letters were published in *America* on July 23, 1960.

In his response to the May editorial, appearing in *America* the following month, Fr. John A. O'Brien praised the editorial board for its vision of providing adequate spiritual care to the students attending secular universities while providing good religious instruction to such students. Fr. O'Brien encouraged the Jesuits to enter this ministry in order to provide scholarly guidance and instruction equal to that of a university faculty.

On June 3, 1960, the National Newman Foundation was incorporated in the District of Columbia "to assist the Bishops of the United States in a most practical way to provide for the members of their flocks attending non-Catholic colleges."[25] The foundation hoped that alumni who benefitted from Newman Clubs while attending university or college would support it financially. The foundation supported eight Newman Institutes of Catholic Thought; student leadership training schools; the Newman chaplains' training schools; and regional projects, such as libraries for individual centers and research projects for the Newman Apostolate.

The following month, on July 9, 1960, *America* reported on the pastoral letter of Archbishop John Ritter of St. Louis, which spelled out three conditions for attendance at non-Catholic colleges:

1. Parents and students must request permission in writing;
2. The chancery should grant the permission only for "just and serious reasons"; and
3. A promise must be made that the student will join the Newman Club or follow some similar program.

DEFINING ROLES—PROMOTING NEWMAN GOALS

The national Newman Association of Faculty and Staff came into being at the annual conference of the federation in Cleveland, Ohio, in September 1960. Created to promote the "spiritual welfare...research and scholarship among Catholic faculty and staff, and to assist the Newman chaplains, students, and alumni on national, province and local levels"[26] the association also sought to provide a medium of communication and exchange of ideas between faculty and staff members of different campuses. Any Catholic faculty or administrator on a secular campus was eligible to be a member of the association.

In early 1960, Newman chaplains debated their role—should they promote formal religious instructions and make religious education their primary goal, or should they emphasize the spiritual and religious development of the student through liturgical practices? The Newman Chaplains' Association advisory board made its decision in July 1961 when they gathered at St. John Seminary in Plymouth, Michigan, agreeing pastoral care should be their primary goal. Although they acknowledged that there would be no Newman Movement without an

---

25 Ibid., 184.
26 Ibid., 126.

educational component, they determined "the essential priestly and pastoral role is the root of our mission to the secular campus."[27]

Fr. John Bradley of Ann Arbor, Michigan, asserted that the Newman Movement had developed beyond that of a club. Due to the appointments of full-time chaplains and new student centers with chapels attached to them, Newman Clubs had become the university parishes. Thus, the same advisory board made the following suggestions to the bishops:

1. Appoint one full-time priest for every three hundred Catholics at residential campuses and for every five hundred on commuter campuses, with another full-time priest for each additional five hundred students in the first situation and one thousand in the second;
2. Notify pastors that if a curate was appointed as part time to this ministry, he has to devote a specific number of hours to the campus; and
3. Provide priests assigned to this ministry with special preparation and training.

Archbishop John Krol, the new moderator of the U.S. Bishops' Youth Department, formally recognized all Newman organizations as official members of the "Newman Family" on April 24, 1962. Archbishop Paul Hallinan of Atlanta (himself a former Newman chaplain) said, "This new structure for the first time officially and formally recognized the Newman Movement as a vigorous arm of the Church in Catholic higher education and a vital apostolate for the Christian formation of students...tomorrow's leaders in the nation and the Church."[28]

Representatives of the Newman Club Federation, chaplains, alumni, and faculty associations were invited to attend the Ann Arbor summit from June 22–24, 1962, at the Gabriel Richard Student Center at the University of Michigan. The goals of the summit were to create a better understanding among all parties involved in the Newman Apostolate and to encourage chaplains, students, faculty, and alumni to work together at state universities and colleges. In order to achieve these goals, Archbishop Hallinan, Newman Club Federation moderator, listed the Newman Movement's five primary tasks:

---

27 Ibid., 124.
28 Ibid., 129.

1. To reach every Catholic student attending a non-Catholic campus;
2. To identify the students with the church on campus;
3. To offer the students a sound religious education program;
4. To provide pastoral care and spiritual formation; and
5. To encourage and form a vigorous leadership for the Catholic lay apostolate.

Looking back, these five primary tasks fulfilled the dreams and vision of Timothy J. Harrington and Fr. John Keogh from the University of Pennsylvania, who served as chaplain of the FCCC from 1917–35. The delegates at the summit concluded that this apostolate was the work of the Catholic Church in the secular campus community.

A 1962 survey indicated that the Newman Apostolate was little known among Catholics and that the apostolate was neither understood nor appreciated. As a result, the chaplains' association and the Newman Foundation agreed to launch a public relations program to educate the Catholic population and promote their goals. Thus, many articles, brochures, and letters to the editor were published in Catholic periodicals and newspapers explaining and promoting the ministry of the movement.

Accompanying this was a significant increase of personnel on the diocesan level as the student population continued to increase on state colleges and universities. In 1962 there were one hundred sixty-nine full-time and approximately six hundred part-time chaplains operating in seventy-nine centers and sixty-five houses. Five years later, the number of full-time chaplains had grown to four hundred twenty-three, with one hundred nine of them also serving as diocesan directors. Seventy-four sisters also worked as Newman chaplains. The number of well-equipped Newman Centers rose to nearly three hundred, and at another fifty-four campuses the Catholic ministry shared ecumenical facilities.

Also in 1962, the National Newman Club Federation (NNCF) felt the need to reprint the *Newman Club Manual*, a handbook for leaders in the Newman Movement, first published in 1954 by Fr. Paul Hallinan, who later became the Archbishop of Atlanta. This fifth edition contained very few revisions, seeming to follow what Fr. Charles Albright, C.S.P., NNCF executive director, had written in the preface of the second edition in March 1959: "The substance of the manual has so proved its value through use that wisdom dictated it would be a waste of time to attempt extensive revisions."

In addition to reprinting the *Newman Club Manual*, the Newman

Foundation financed a series of Newman chaplains' training schools. The first one took place in Ann Arbor for four weeks; moved to Minneapolis, Minnesota, for the next two years; and to Boulder, Colorado, for three more years. In 1967, the Frank J. Lewis Foundation, recognizing the importance of new chaplains' training, funded two Newman chaplains' schools, one in the East at Harvard, and the other in the West in Boulder. According to the brochure, "The Newman Chaplains School intends to fulfill a long-felt need by offering basic preparation to the young priest who is assigned to care for Catholic students on a secular campus." The foundation provided forty scholarships. Through the generous support of this foundation, the Frank J. Lewis Institute for Campus Ministry Orientation has been held almost every year since then.

Besides financing chaplains' training schools, the Newman Foundation also supported student leadership training schools; Newman Institutes of Catholic Thought; and the international desk of the apostolate, which opened in 1965 under the directorship of Maryknoll Fr. Laurence T. Murphy.

As Catholic institutions evaluated their role and mission to the student population in the 1960s, officials of the college and university section of the National Catholic Educational Association (NCEA) began to look at the importance of the Newman Movement at their 1962 meeting. The private professional organization founded in 1904 represents Catholic educators who serve students in Catholic schools, including colleges and universities, students in religious education programs, and seminarians. NCEA officials realized that Newman Centers and Clubs were not in competition with Catholic college education and acknowledged these centers addressed the spiritual and pastoral needs of the students attending secular institutions.

At the 1963 NCEA meeting, former Newman chaplain and now Archbishop Hallinan told the delegates that the time had come that every Catholic student, regardless of the school he or she attended, should be included when defining Catholic higher education. The Newman ministry benefitted by comments such as these and from previous editorials in the Jesuit weekly *America*.

Occidental College, Los Angeles (1962–69)

My first task when I went to Occidental College was to find a Catholic professor to serve as the club advisor. Dr. Fisher, an English professor and a convert to the Catholic Church, accepted the invitation without hesitation. With his help, we started to reach out to Catholic students. I also started to learn my role as a campus minister. We had a few Catholics attending a weekly bible study, and I believed we could get more participation from Catholic students if we celebrated the Sunday Eucharist on campus. After a lengthy correspondence and discussions with James Francis Cardinal McIntyre, Archbishop of Los Angeles, Occidental College President Coons, and later President Gilmore, permission was given to celebrate the Mass on Sundays on campus. Herrick Chapel on the campus of Occidental College, which was a Presbyterian institution, was ideal for Catholic liturgy. I announced that Mass would be celebrated every Sunday at 5:00 p.m. and was amazed at the number of Catholic students who turned up for the first Mass.

It was during this time that changes in the liturgy ordained by the Second Vatican Council were taking place. I held a series of talks on the development of the Mass so that the students would have a better understanding of the changes that were taking place. We were also the first Catholic community in the Archdiocese of Los Angeles to introduce contemporary music.

Campus ministry has been an advocate for social justice since its beginning. During the height of the civil rights movement, I discovered that housing for African-American students attending Occidental College was a big problem because discrimination was prevalent in the 1960s. Once I discovered this problem, I wanted to act on it. I asked myself, why is a person discriminated against because of his/her color? After consultation with some parishioners and college students, we decided to ask the parishioners of St. Dominic to sign an open housing petition. A few parishioners were vehemently opposed, but with God's grace, the majority signed in favor. So African-American students began to be treated as their white classmates. Justice prevailed. And after seven years at Occidental College, I moved on.

During my time at Occidental College, in August 1965, I recall our provincial, Fr. Joseph Agius, O.P., called the very first meeting of all the Dominicans of the Western Province who were active in campus ministry. We met at our summer house at St. Benedict's Lodge in McKenzie Bridge, Oregon. We shared our involvement in this ministry that the Province had started to undertake. Since then our Province has made a commitment to Campus Ministry. After that meeting, many Dominicans also got involved in events, committees, and boards on the national, regional and local levels.

NEW AWAKENINGS AND NEW CONFLICTS

In September 19, 1964, two young Jesuits, Richard J. Clifford and William R. Callahan, wrote an article *in America* on "Catholics in Higher Education—A Study of the Next 20 years."[29] In this article the authors acknowledged the importance of Newman chaplaincies in state colleges and universities since more Catholics are attending these state colleges and universities than Catholic institutions: "In the academic year 1963–64, approximately 4,530,000 students were enrolled in the colleges and universities of the United States. Recent studies indicate that Catholics are attending college in proportion to their share of the general population (23.5 percent); so we may conclude that about 1,070,000 of these students were Catholic." They predicted that "the Catholic student segment will swell from a 1960 total of 830,000 to a 1985 figure of 2.9 million students. Where will they be educated?"[30]

They pointed out that "the steadily increasing Catholic enrollment on secular campuses—and the increase of Catholic faculty members—offers one of the greatest opportunities of the modern church to bring Christ' teaching and example to men." Thus they proposed that "on these secular campuses, the ideal Catholic center would be not merely a social organization, but rather one built around the rapidly developing group-concept of a Catholic center...staffed by a group whose talents and interests included the faculty-member scholar, the pastor and counselor as well as the administrator of the center."[31] Thus such a center will help the educated Catholic on a secular campus with an opportunity to know their faith fully and practice it actively. "To allow 80 percent of the best educated Catholics to shift for themselves spiritually or receive minimal seems completely unacceptable."[32] They strongly suggested that "the intellectual training of the religious orders devoted to higher education makes their priests particularly apt for this apostolate."[33]

This was something the founders of the Newman Movement had urged. However, although members of religious orders were encouraged to undertake such a ministry, the Newman Apostolate remained almost exclusively the ministry of diocesan priests in the early 1960s. According

---

29 *America*, 19 September 1964, 288.
30 Ibid., 288.
31 Ibid., 290–291.
32 Ibid., 291.
33 Ibid., 291.

to the 1965–66 Newman annual report, two hundred six religious priests and eighty-six sisters from various religious orders and congregations were chaplains on secular campuses, while two hundred seventy-two full-time and eight hundred seventy-six part-time chaplains were diocesan clergy.

During the turbulent '60s, the student federation lost significant membership. By the mid-1960s, the student section of the NNCF was on the verge of collapse as national membership declined. Even on the local scene, although more Catholics were enrolling in state universities, the attendance of students at religious functions decreased. Dissatisfaction with a full-time salaried national president who was not a student, too many cliques, and lack of social awareness were some of the reasons that contributed to the decline of the membership and, eventually, of the federation.

Conflict between students and the clergy burst into the open in June 1965. Newman activists questioned the control of the NCWC Youth Department. Federation President Julius Gilbertson issued a proclamation of emancipation in which he proposed a pro-student movement that would operate outside Church structures but within the spirit of the Church. In this way, he argued, the laity would emerge as responsible and mature leaders. Students also feared that the bishops would control the federation. When the chaplains' advisory board met in June 1964 to deal with this crisis, they passed a resolution that gave more autonomy to the students, at least in relation to the Youth Department.

The officers of the Newman Student Federation, after several meetings with representatives of Protestant and Orthodox student groups, in September 1966 decided to join together to form the University Christian Movement. In doing so, the leaders failed to consult their membership, their chaplains, or the NCWC department. After much thought, discussion, and prayer a Catholic Commission on the Church in the American University was created. Ten chaplains and twenty students were asked to evaluate the Newman Apostolate in light of the Second Vatican Council (1962–1965) and the changes that were taking place in the university world. The Newman Movement felt that the Second Vatican Council confirmed belief in its ideals such as the emergence of the laity, ecumenical outreach, liturgical renewal, freedom of conscience, and collegiality.

In the midst of all the turmoil that was going on in the Newman Movement, the Newman Federation held a congress in Dallas, Texas, in August 1966. It came at an appropriate time to save the movement. Episcopal moderator, Bishop James W. Malone of the Diocese of Youngstown, Ohio, promoted the restructuring of the apostolate. He called for innovation and decentralization, especially in light of the need to adapt the work of the Church to differing conditions among colleges and universities. He insisted that the apostolate existed primarily for the students, adding that any section not fulfilling the mission of the apostolate should either change or cease to exist.

In March 1967 at the Maryknoll Seminary in Glen Ellyn, Illinois, the commission redefined the Newman Apostolate from the "work of the Church in the secular campus community" into a "searching, believing, loving, worshiping…presence of the Catholic Church in the campus community."[34] This presence included ecumenical relations and dedication to social justice issues. The commission also favored the establishment of diocesan boards instead of provincial and national structures. To finance the national office, each Newman entity was asked to tithe one percent of its annual budget.

A counter-conference led by some leaders of the student federation in July 1967 in Hyattsville, Maryland, opposed the Glen Ellyn proposals. They maintained that the proposals would destroy the student movement as a lay organization and reduce it to just a managerial agency. But the following month, at the congress of the Newman Apostolate held at Northern Illinois University in DeKalb, the commission's recommendations were overwhelmingly accepted.

For many years, the student federation had preserved the dream and the momentum of the apostolate. Unfortunately, with the collapse of the University Christian Movement, the Newman Student Federation fell apart in 1969. Fr. Jack Bendik, from the Diocese of Scranton, Pennsylvania, recalled the demise of the student federation in his keynote address to the National Catholic Student Coalition conference on January 6, 1988:

> I was invited to participate along with my students in a National Newman Congress to be held at Rutgers University/ Douglas College Campus in New Brunswick, New Jersey. There were 556 registered guests from 43 states and the District of Columbia. … It was FANTASTIC!…The shocking thing about

---

34 Evans, *The Newman Movement*, 164.

all that happened at that conference is that on August 28, 1968, an editorial appeared in the *DAILY RAG*, a mini paper published during the conference. It decried the increased cost of the national Newman structure, and hailed it as ineffective and cumbersome. The editor, Kathleen Okenica, wrote: 'If no definitive decision on structure is reached this afternoon, the aging Commission will continue to age. Why not tie all the loose ends once and for all? Let's not just let the national structure of Newman shrivel up and slowly die. Let's kill it altogether.' Later that day, the delegates voted to abolish the National Newman Structure stating that any structure as such will exist on the local, diocesan and regional levels.[35]

As the student federation was falling apart, in 1969 the United States Catholic Conference (USCC), which had replaced the NCWC, set up a Department of Christian Education that included a Division of Campus Ministry with a full-time priest-director and a sister as his full-time assistant. The new division was recognized as an educational agency, and for the first time it was included in the annual budget of the bishops' conference. That same year, the Knights of Columbus gave $50,000 to Washington's Center for Applied Research in the Apostolate (CARA) to open a Department of Campus Ministry to help with the future planning, training, and performance of campus ministers, which was advantageous for the Newman Movement.

NEW ASSOCIATION

At a 1967 meeting of the NNCA in New Orleans, the chaplains passed a resolution for the association to "evolve into a professional organization concerned with continuing discussion and development of the work of the Chaplains at the University."[36] This decision was discussed in the 1971 annual report given by Fr. Raymond Sullivan, chair of the executive board of the Catholic Campus Ministry Association (CCMA), the organization that developed as a result of that 1967 resolution. Fr. Sullivan continued in the annual report:

---

35 Jack Bendick, Keynote Address at the National Catholic Student Coalition Conference, 6 January 1988.

36 Raymond Sullivan, *1971 Annual Report of the Catholic Campus Ministry Association.*

The fuller sense of that motion was described in the following words: That the new form be organized along professional lines; an organization which is characterized by self-determination of the chaplains themselves, as a body; an organization which chooses its own leadership, which is totally self-supporting. An organization which meets according to the will of the membership to exchange studies relating to the profession and which commissions studies for the growth of the work and communication within itself and outside itself to the broader community which it serves; an organization which avoids, as much as possible, the complexities of organization, which seems to have simple structure in order to expend its energies towards the growth of the group in self-understanding, promoting projects of study and action, conveying the mind and conclusions of the whole body to other groups, as well as fostering a relationship between its membership and that of other related professional associations.[37]

After the 1967 meeting, a commission was set up to restructure the association. The constitution committee reported that ballots had been sent by mail that indicated overwhelming support for the new constitution. At the annual meeting of campus ministers held in 1969 in Detroit, the Newman chaplains unanimously adopted the new constitution and by-laws for the association, which a hard-working committee had put together in a tedious meeting at O'Hare Inn in Chicago in November 1968. After the approval of the constitution, "our (Executive Board) efforts have been directed toward fostering an evolution towards a truly professional organization which could best serve the membership."[38]

Since the chaplains adopted a new constitution without holding elections, they decided to keep the officers of the NNCA as the officers of the new CCMA; the officers were asked to act in that capacity for one year, thereby completing the term of office in which they were elected under the old constitution. The first members of the CCMA executive board were Fr. Charles Forsyth, O.S.B., chair; Fr. Robert Bullock; Fr.

---

37 Ibid.
38 Catholic Campus Ministry Association Newsletter, Vols. 1,3, July 1971.

Philip Baron; Fr. Leo Piguet; Fr. Charles Borgognoni; and Sr. Sheila Doherty. Because the West was not represented on the executive board, in 1970 the board appointed Fr. Patrick LaBelle, O.P., as a voting member of the committee to represent the Western United States.

The new by-laws listed the following standing committees:

1. Program committee for continuing education;
2. Committee for orientation of campus ministry personnel;
3. Committee for coordinating ecumenical affairs;
4. Committee for commuter and community colleges;
5. Committee for liturgical affairs;
6. Committee for long-range planning; and
7. Nominations committee to be named by the executive board at the fall meeting.

From the very beginning, the association relied heavily on volunteers (as it still does). In a letter sent to all campus ministers in October 1969, Fr. Leo Piguet, the secretary-treasurer, urged "in order to continue the progress already made by this infant organization, it is essential that our standing committees function fruitfully. Please note the enclosed membership application form with committees listed on the bottom of the form. Check one of these committees if you have interest and the time to give."[39] Membership dues were $20 per individual, and an associate membership cost $10.

The newly formed CCMA had about three hundred fifty chaplains as members with a budget of $15,000. The new organization developed national workshops and other training programs in order to help experienced campus ministers in various fields, such as ministry at community colleges and with minority groups and the training of peer ministers and others. Fr. Laurence Murphy, M.M., the director of the USSC's Division of Campus Ministry, helped CCMA in offering two annual training schools for the newly appointed campus ministers.

Following the opinion of most chaplains, Fr. Murphy proposed two new developments. First, he suggested enabling chaplains on Catholic and secular campuses to work together more closely through membership in CCMA and under the guidance of local diocesan directors. Second, he proposed the organization of diocesan directors in order to support and

---

39 Letter from Leo Piguet to potential members of CCMA, October 1969.

prepare professionally the leadership of the organization and to clarify
the role of the diocesan directors in view of the needs of the apostolate.[40]

The new association had to tackle three large issues:

1. The commuter-community school situation with particular
   attention paid to practical concerns;
2. The relationship between CCMA and the National Campus
   Ministry Association (NCMA), a Protestant organization similar
   to the structure of CCMA; and
3. The proposed National Training Center in Boston for campus
   ministry personnel.

At the annual business meeting of CCMA held in March 31, 1970,
in the Traymore Hotel in Atlantic City, New Jersey, Fr. Robert Bullock
and Fr. Laurence Murphy addressed the eighty-three campus ministers
present about a proposed training center in Boston for campus ministry
personnel. In September 1969, Fr. Murphy had met with representatives
from higher education and campus ministry. The consensus of this group
was that a more systematic, sophisticated avenue for preparing campus
ministers ought to be available. The USCC had approved the center and
its funding at its April 1970 meeting

The National Center for Campus Ministry opened in the fall
of 1971 in Boston, which was chosen because of its diverse campus
ministry situations. The basic functions of the center would be: 1)
residential training of campus ministry personnel; 2) continuing
education of campus ministry personnel; and 3) research and publication.
The Newman Foundation gave a $5,000 grant to the new center.[41]
Unfortunately the center did not last very long.

Recognizing the need to have professional campus ministers, in
1973, Fr. Charles Forsyth, O.S.B., the first chair of CCMA, established
a master's degree program for campus ministry at Fordham University
for "lay people, religious and clergy who are interested in or have
some experience in ministry on the college campus."[42] It appeared the
Newman Movement had returned to its origins, with a diocesan-centered
concept having the backing of a national office. The educational mission

---

40 Rev. Laurence Murphy, M.M., to diocesan directors of campus ministry, 31 October 1969.

41 CCMA annual meeting report, March 1970.

42 Catholic Campus Ministry Association, Brochure announcing graduate program at Fordham
University.

of the Newman Apostolate was endorsed by the Vatican II document "Declaration on Christian Education," although it fell short of giving the full support for which Newman chaplains had hoped. Bishops were now supportive of the work of campus ministers. Bishop Hugh A. Donohoe of Stockton, California, urged his fellow bishops to promote Newman chaplaincies and centers as generously and as zealously as they did parish schools.

Addressing the major issue of ecumenism, and living within the spirit of Vatican II, CCMA established a very good working relationship with the National Campus Ministry Association (NCMA), a Protestant organization whose purpose was to amalgamate many denominational campus ministry organizations. After several discussions between the executive boards of both organizations, Fr. Piguet reported on March 24, 1970, that the executive board of NCMA unanimously agreed to a proposal made by the CCMA executive board for automatic co-membership between NCMA and CCMA upon payment of dues to only one organization, allowing any individual to hold full membership in both groups if he or she so desired.

The July 1971 CCMA newsletter announced that CCMA and NCMA would hold their first jointly sponsored programs for campus ministers. Titled "Consultations on Prophetic Inquiry in Campus Ministry," two four-day workshops were held—one in Pittsburgh and the other in Denver. A $25 registration fee included room, board, and materials. The purpose of the consultations focused on two questions. The first was how ministries in higher education could implement prophetic inquiry as a mode of ministry, and the second was how Christian ministry to higher education assists the university in understanding its own ministry of service. The two organizations also co-sponsored ecumenical institutes in Cuernavaca, Mexico.

The NCEA established a Commission on Campus Ministry in 1970, which carried the possibility of mutual cooperation between campus ministers of both Catholic and secular institutions. A special session on campus ministry was hosted in April 1971 at the annual convention of the NCEA in Minneapolis where Fr. Ray Sullivan, CCMA president, and Fr. Jim Blumeyer, S.J., coordinator of religious activities at Rockhurst College in Kansas City, shared their own experiences and the problems they faced in their respective arenas. They were determined to put aside their former differences and unite in a common effort, which was a dream come true for pioneers such as Fr. Peter Edward Dietz, chaplain at Oberlin College in Ohio in 1907, who predicted that someday all rivalry between the two camps would be erased and the two would work together hand in hand in "one mighty stream."[43] Setting aside former differences, campus ministers in public and church-related institutions began collaborating. Bishops and campus ministers dedicated themselves to the common effort of promoting the presence of the church on all campuses.

Early 1970s reports from CARA and the USCC's Division of Campus Ministry gave a very healthy picture of campus ministry. There were 1,450 chaplains, 80 of whom were sisters, on approximately 1,200 campuses. Of the priests, 500 were appointed full time, one-third had canonical status as pastors or associate pastors, more than one-fifth of the chaplains served on ecumenical teams, and about eighty percent of them regarded campus ministry as a career itself. About four hundred chaplains received direct diocesan grants, while most of the other Newman Centers' financial support came from other sources such as alumni or parents of students. More than three-fourths of the priests provided religious services on weekends, and about two-thirds celebrated daily Mass. Two-thirds of the campus ministers organized social activities on a regular basis and offered religious instruction, and about half of the priests indicated that they were involved in social action movements on their campuses.

Retreats or Christian weekends were also successful in many campus ministry settings. The 1970 CARA report on sisters in campus ministry indicated that the sisters who worked as campus ministers considered themselves to be professional ministers who performed many valuable roles such as teaching classes, leading discussion groups, counseling, organizing student religious and welfare programs, assisting with liturgical planning and celebrations, marriage preparation, and preaching. They were well accepted by the students and the entire campus. In June 1971, a new CCMA committee was established for Women Religious in Campus Ministry, and Ann Kelly was appointed as chairman. This was another attempt to serve the specific needs of women in the ministry.[44]

The 1970s saw the professional growth of the role of diocesan directors of campus ministry as well, which was another major development in the structure of campus ministry. Experienced diocesan

---

43 Evans, *The Newman Movement*, 171.

44 CCMA newsletter, Vol. 1,3, July 1971.

directors were now able to prepare their own handbooks and other aids. Steps were underway to organize a national board to facilitate communication, develop policy, and speed up the needed expansion, both locally and nationally.

Another phenomenon took place in the mid-1970s. With the empowerment of the laity in the Church through the teachings of the Second Vatican Council, lay persons were appointed as campus ministers. Dr. Michael Galligan-Stierle, then campus minister at Barry University in Miami, Florida, chaired a lay ministry task force that conducted national research and wrote theological "white papers" on the acceptability of lay ministry. Jennifer Konecny, campus minister at Santa Clara University, was the first lay person elected to the National executive board in 1976; the following year, she became first lay person and the first woman to be elected CCMA president. She was followed by another lay person, Dr. Robert Ludwig, campus minister at De Paul University in Chicago, who served as CCMA president from 1978–79. Since then, the laity has been an important factor in campus ministry and has served the membership in various capacities at national, regional, and local levels.

As the association grew, so did the workload of the CCMA president. In 1977, Sr. Margaret Ivers, I.B.V.M., was hired as its first full-time executive director. The first executive office was established at Wayne State University in Detroit; the main office was later relocated to the University of Dayton in Ohio. Mr. Don McCrabb succeeded Sr. Ivers in 1985. Mr. Ed Franchi was appointed CCMA executive director in 1998, and Sr. Joan Mikulski followed Ed for a couple of months in 2007 before resigning. Rev. Martin O. Moran, former chaplain at Bucknell University, took over as executive director on June 1, 2007. In 2001 the CCMA executive board voted to relocate the office to Cincinnati as they recognized the need for expansion in order to meet the needs of its members. Under the leadership of the executive directors and the hard work of every national executive board throughout the years, CCMA became a recognized entity in the U.S. church.

At the prompting of Fr. Joe Kenna, the USCC director of campus ministry, diocesan directors began exploring the formation of their own association. Although diocesan directors met annually for many years, it was not until their meeting in Boston on November 9–10, 1982, after long hours of public debate and many private discussions, that the National Association of Diocesan Directors of Campus Ministry (NADDCM) was formally established in order to support and facilitate the development of campus ministry in the dioceses. Fr. Vincent Krische, director of the Newman Center at the University of Kansas in Lawrence, was elected the first president. In 1969, Fr. Murphy had already told the diocesan directors that they "should have a strong voice and could make significant contributions."[45] So, Fr. Kenna continued to build on Fr. Murphy's hard work with diocesan directors: "As the church's ministry to higher education continues to gain greater importance in our country, it is necessary for us to establish a viable structure enabling us to meet the needs and demands of our university communities."[46] The following year, the diocesan directors met in Madison to celebrate the 100th anniversary of the birth of the pre-Newman Movement, the Melvin Club.

University of California, Riverside (1972–1976)

After seven years at Occidental College, I was appointed student master for the Dominican seminarians at St. Albert Priory in Oakland, California. So in October of 1969, I went to St. Albert. Three years later, I returned to campus ministry when I was asked by Provincial Fr. Paul Scanlon, O.P., to go to the University of California, Riverside, to help out because one of the chaplains was sick. After a few weeks there, I was appointed co-director of the St. Andrew's Catholic Newman Center, which was housed at an ecumenical center called Watkins House. Since there was little participation from the students, it was very challenging for me to build a student community. But as I started to get to know some students, they invited me to visit their residence halls. Before I knew it, we had a small community on campus. I celebrated Masses in student housing and held discussion groups and bible studies in the residence halls. The students were very instrumental in developing the growth of the Newman Club on campus, and they were the best public relations for the Catholic Newman community.

I have always admired the enthusiasm of the students, and I believe in empowering them. The Dominicans were also entrusted to minister to the students at Riverside City College. I encouraged the students to find a house near the college to facilitate our ministry to them. One evening around 9:30, the doorbell of our Dominican house rang, and I was confronted by three excited community college students. They had found a house across the street from campus that would make a perfect Newman Center. The following day

---

45 Rev. Laurence Murphy, M.M., to diocesan directors of campus ministry, 31 October 1969.
46 Rev. Joseph Kenna to diocesan directors of campus ministry, 17 November 1982.

I went to see the house and the landlord; later that day, I signed a lease. Our Newman sponsors, a lay group interested in campus ministry, supported the house financially, and thus began a very vital ministry to the community college students. The most popular event was the TBTGIF Mass—Thanks Be to God It's Friday Mass. Students, staff, and faculty attended this weekly liturgy at 2:00 p.m.

One of the most active groups at the Newman Center was the CIA— Catholics in Action—who focused on social justice issues. Once a month we gathered for a pot-luck dinner and planning. At one of our meetings, we decided to host a dinner/dance for the shut-ins and the elderly who lived alone. We were inspired by the teaching of Jesus that "when you hold a lunch or dinner, do not invite your friends or your brothers or your relatives or your wealthy neighbor...rather invite the poor...because of their inability to repay you."[47] The whole Newman community pulled together and for three years held a fabulous dinner/dance for more than eighty elderly and shut-ins.

In 1976, Watkins House was scheduled to be turned over to the university, so the Newman community had to find another location for worship, gatherings, and offices. After a long search, we found a two-story building that at one time had been a pizza/bar. That year, I left campus ministry in order to be the Director of Adult Education and the Charismatic Renewal for the north counties of Diocese of San Diego. When the Diocese of San Diego was divided in July 1978 and a new Diocese of San Bernardino was created, the newly appointed Bishop Phillip Straling asked me to continue as Director of Adult Education and the Charismatic Renewal for the diocese. I did not leave campus ministry completely, since I celebrated Sunday Masses at UC Riverside and California State University, San Bernardino, on many weekends.

THE PASTORAL LETTER ON CATHOLIC HIGHER EDUCATION AND THE PASTORAL MISSION OF THE CHURCH

After the Second Vatican Council, Catholic campus ministry on Catholic colleges and universities became more organized. The National Conference of Catholic Bishops (NCCB) addressed the role of campus ministry on Catholic campuses in their pastoral letter "Catholic Higher

---

47 Luke 14:12–14.

Education and the Pastoral Mission of the Church." The bishops made it clear that campus ministry on Catholic colleges and universities "should not and cannot be limited to persons formally designated as campus ministers even though they are rightfully expected to take the lead."[48] They continued, "The pastoral document envisions a Catholic university or college as an enterprise wholly committed to evangelical ministry."[49] The letter insists that "trustees, administrators, faculties, parents and above all students, need to see their whole college or university experiences a unique opportunity for the discovery of God's abiding presence and influence in the lives of people and in the signs of the times. At most and at best an office of campus ministry can be a catalyst to spark and to energize the total institution's involvement in a gospel-oriented evangelism."[50] They further stated that campus ministry should not include just the elements of a parish ministry, but instead should also be a voice at the policy-making level and to insist in season and out of season on the preservation and enrichment of the institution's religious tradition.[51]

At the end of this statement on campus ministry in Catholic higher education, the bishops added a footnote: "Since this message has addressed exclusively Catholic higher education, we were unable to speak of the excellent intellectual and pastoral leadership of many Catholics engaged as teachers, administrators, and campus ministers in colleges and universities which are not Catholic. We hope for a future opportunity to speak of their invaluable contribution to the intellectual life of the country."[52]

Arizona State University, Tempe, Arizona (1980–86)

After living for eight years in Riverside, in 1980 I was assigned to be the Director of All Saints Catholic Newman Center serving Arizona State University in Tempe, Arizona—one of the largest state universities in the country. I accepted the challenge to serve a very large Catholic community compared to the one at UC Riverside. The first weekend I celebrated Mass,

---

48 National Conference of Catholic Bishops, Catholic Higher Education and the Pastoral Mission of the Church (Washington, DC: United States Catholic Conference, 1981), par. 50.

49 Ibid., par. 44.

50 Ibid., par. 45.

51 Ibid,, par. 47 and 46.

52 Ibid. footnote 32 to par. 64.

Fr. Thomas De Man, O.P., my predecessor, and I gave each other a blessing at all the Masses. For me, it was very moving. I experienced a warm welcome from the community. I can say that the Dominicans and Fr. Tom had built a very strong, lively, and exciting community. I was surprised to see so many students attending Sunday Masses. Good liturgical music attracted the students; in fact, a good number of our musicians who played music at the weekend Masses at the Center, including Jaime Cortez, Paul Hillebrand, and Tim and Julie Smith, now write music for Oregon Catholic Press.

One of the problems I faced—if one can call it a problem—was that the chapel was too small to accommodate all of our Sunday worshippers. We had to turn students away because of lack of space. It took me a couple of years before I figured out how to expand the Center in order to hold more people. With the help of Fred Bersch, a construction engineering student, we knocked down walls and installed garage doors between the chapel and the lobby, so that on Sundays we could open the doors and put chairs in the lobby for people who would be attending the Masses. Besides the remodeling of the Center, I continued to make improvements in the Old Church, the first church built in the Valley of the Sun, which was reopened by my predecessor, Fr. Tom.

I have always been energized to see the involvement of the students and the whole community. The enthusiasm of a few rubbed off on many other students, and I believe students are the best evangelizers on campus. I inherited a large Charismatic group; people from all over the Valley attended our prayer group, and it was a blessing for the Newman community to have such a group. I knew that those people prayed for the Newman community every day. Many students participated in retreats, which were led by the chaplains and the students. Directing retreats is not my talent, but I am a good supporter. I remember the big headache it always was to find transportation for the students and young adults to get to the retreat centers. I believed in these retreats, because I saw firsthand the impact they had on the students—many came back from a weekend retreat with a true change of heart.

Besides the students, campus ministers are called to reach out to faculty and staff. We had a monthly luncheon with a speaker for university faculty, staff, and administration. They were very well attended, and I personally enjoyed getting to know the faculty, staff and administration. The attendance of university members at the celebration of the Mass and other events sponsored by the Newman Center was a great example for our students, especially because they had enough professors who were openly hostile to *all religious beliefs. It was a great opportunity for students to meet their professors outside the classroom.*

A good number of male students asked me to establish a council of the Knights of Columbus at the Center. In a few months we were able to gather more than thirty students in order to establish a council. On May 3, 1982, St. Thomas Aquinas Council 8090 was established. The Knights of Columbus principles are fraternity, charity, unity, and patriotism. The council was a great help to me and the community.

Once again I found myself involved in another movement—the Sanctuary Movement. In the mid-80s, when political violence was taking place in El Salvador and Nicaragua, about five hundred religious congregations helped Central American refugees and offered them sanctuary. Considering the need to help these refugees, the Newman community held a number of meetings to study the issue and determine whether we would offer sanctuary to these refugees. After prayer, reflection, and discernment, the community voted overwhelmingly to give shelter to refugees, and on May 11, 1985, the Newman community, in a public prayer service, declared the Center a Sanctuary, giving shelter to an El Salvadorian family. It was very moving to see our community embracing this El Salvadorian family. In response to the Newman Center action, Bishop Thomas O'Brien, then Bishop of Phoenix, said, "The people who covenanted together at the Newman Center seem to me to be offering humanitarian help to refugees who, in many cases, should be helped with the cooperation of the Immigration and Naturalization Service."

When I think of the bold decision the Newman community took in declaring the Center a sanctuary, I always thank God for giving me the courage to step out in faith and say "YES, we will be a sanctuary," in spite of the opposition of some church leaders. It was a great experience for the students to learn that no matter what one's nationality is, we are all called to take care of the needs of one another. We are all brothers and sisters in Christ.

PASTORAL LETTER ON CAMPUS MINISTRY

In the spring of 1981, Fr. Joe Kenna, the bishops' representative for campus ministry at the NCCB, was called by the National Advisory Committee to address some concerns about campus ministry. Fr. Kenna reminded the committee of the footnote at the very end of the pastoral letter "Catholic Higher Education and Pastoral Mission of the Church." The National Advisory Committee picked up the idea and voted to ask the bishops to write a letter addressing campus ministry at public and private colleges and universities.

In order to fulfill their promise, the bishops selected a committee with Bishop William B. Friend of Alexandria/Shreveport, Louisiana, as chair. The committee met for the first time in the spring of 1983 after the U.S. bishops gave their approval to write the letter. The committee engaged Fr. Jim Bacik, pastor of Corpus Christi University Parish in Toledo, Ohio, to draft the letter. Several drafts were presented as a result of a wide range of consultations. The committee sifted through, evaluated, and organized the results of the many suggestions presented to them by bishops, diocesan directors of campus ministry, campus ministers, university presidents, academic vice presidents, faculty, and thousands of students.

A draft of a pastoral letter titled "The Quest for Wisdom: The Church in Dialogue with Higher Education" was rejected. After more consultation, on November 15, 1985, a new chapter in the history of campus ministry took place when the pastoral letter "Empowered by the Spirit: Campus Ministry Faces the Future" was accepted by the U.S. bishops.

This letter became the roadmap for campus ministry in the United States. In it, the bishops identify six aspects for campus ministers "that flow from the nature of the Church and the situation on campus":

1. Forming the faith community;
2. Appropriating the faith;
3. Forming the Christian conscience;
4. Educating for justice;
5. Facilitating personal development; and
6. Developing leaders for the future.[53]

In this letter the bishops gave principles and strategies for campus ministry, and the letter highlights the bishops' own responsibilities to "serve the Church on campus" and "calls the Church to an exciting new phase in the history of campus ministry in our country."

---

53 NCCB, Empowered by the Spirit: Campus Ministry Faces the Future (Washington, DC: United States Conference of Catholic Bishops, 1985), par. 5.

This letter opened the way for further discussion and development. In November 1987, Bro. Peter Clifford, the USCC representative for campus ministry and higher education, invited twelve campus ministers to dinner in an effort to solicit suggestions on furthering campus ministry nationwide and on implementing the bishops' pastoral letter. The group endorsed the idea of creating a campus ministry handbook of resources; as a result *The Gospel on Campus: A Handbook of Campus Ministry Programs and Resources* was created, and the first edition was published in 1991, selling more than 6,000 copies. An edited second edition was printed in 1996.

Educational opportunities for campus ministers were and are still available. In 1985 the U.S. bishops created the campus ministry mentoring program under the first director, Susan Spadinger. The purpose of this new program was to facilitate new campus ministers in their ministry. East and West study weeks, national conventions, regional conferences, retreats, and leadership workshops for campus ministers sponsored by CCMA, NADDCM, USCCB, and the National Catholic Student Coalition (NCSC) have been convened on a regular basis.

University of Oregon, Eugene, Oregon (1987–1993)

When I finished my assignment at Arizona State University, I took a one-year sabbatical to retool. I was fortunate to spend three months in Israel and Egypt. It was also the first time I was able to be with my family for an extended period of time after 25 years in the States. In the middle of my sabbatical, Provincial Fr. John Flannery, O.P., asked me to go to serve the community at the University of Oregon. I was reluctant to go because the weather does not agree with me. I am warm-blooded person! But the provincial reminded me that I joined the whole province, not just the Southwest. So, from a Sun Devil I became a Duck—at least I was still in the Pac-10 (now the Pac-12). When I arrived in Oregon, the football coach asked me to celebrate Mass for the team, a tradition that the team had for many years. It was started by then Coach Len Casanova. I also had the honor to celebrate Mass for the football team and their supporters when the Ducks played at the Rose Bowl on January 2, 1995.

For six years I tolerated the weather—the gray skies, the drizzle, and the rain. I realized how much I missed the blue skies and the warm temperatures of the Southwest. But it is the people who make the Center. We had a very generous faith community that was very much involved in all aspects of the life of the community. I had great admiration for a group of parishioners who not only promoted social justice but really lived it. They were great models for the student community. The mixture of the young, the middle-aged, and the elders created a great community because they were able to learn from one another and support one another.

In Eugene, I was not only the pastor of the Catholic university community but also a landlord for forty-five students who lived together at Chelsea House, which the Newman Center rented from a sorority. It was very efficiently run by students under the supervision of the Newman staff. The Chelsea House students were the driving force behind the many activities held for the community. Every Wednesday at 9:00 p.m. we gathered for the celebration of the Mass. Many times a student would give a reflection on the scripture reading of the day. Even in Eugene, retreats were very popular with the students. We took advantage of the Dominican retreat house on the McKenzie River, a wonderful retreat site.

As a pastor, one not only takes care of the spiritual needs of the community, but one also takes care of the facilities. One has to like administration, overseeing the property, and raising funds. During my time in Eugene, I raised funds in order to replace the squeaky floor of the chapel, put in new carpet, install better lighting in the sanctuary area, and replace the rail for the physically challenged.

As discussed previously, campus ministers have their own association, which was founded in 1969, and I have been a member since the beginning. In 1989, we held the first convention in New Orleans. I was asked to chair the second one, held at the Fairmont in San Jose, California, in January 1992. I felt honored to be asked to take on such a task. Besides the usual care of the Newman Center, I had to plan the conference with the help of a national committee. It was a great opportunity for me to get to know many of my colleagues throughout the United States, and I later became involved on the national executive board of CCMA for six years and NADCCM for another six years.

THE FIRST OF SEVERAL HAPPENINGS

The first national convention chaired by Sr. Sarah Landis, I.H.M., took place January 2–5, 1989, at the Fairmont Hotel in New Orleans. This convention was preceded by East and West study weeks for campus ministers held every year for many years in Florida and California.

Another important event to educate students and campus ministers was the creation of the Campus Ministry Leadership Institute, which started in the summer of 1998 and was held at the University of Notre Dame in South Bend, Indiana, under the leadership of Dr. Michael Galligan-Stierle and a team of professional campus ministers and student leader instructors.

To emphasize the professionalism of campus ministers, the USCC Commission on Certification and Accreditation approved CCMA's certification standards in 1992. The following May, the CCMA executive board appointed the first national certification committee, which began its certification program with an open "grandparenting" process for those who had been active in the association for the previous seven years. The certification, which is valid for seven years, is "a distinction for a campus minister signifying a high level of competence, as well as significant personal, theological and spiritual reflection."[54]

The tenth anniversary of the bishops' pastoral letter on campus ministry did not go unnoticed. A couple of actions marked this anniversary. First, a symposium for Catholic bishops and campus ministry leaders took place at Washington Court Hotel in Washington, D.C., on September 10, 1995, to celebrate the anniversary and to discuss "The Church's Presence in the University and in University Culture," a letter issued on June 4, 1994, by the Vatican Congregation for Catholic Education and the Pontifical Councils for the Laity and Culture. At this gathering, sponsored by CCMA, NADDCM, and NCSC, various speakers addressed an important issue for campus ministers: "Religious Literacy and College Students: The Promise of Campus Ministry." Don McCrabb, then CCMA executive director, stated that this symposium was "only one step in a much larger effort to engage all Catholics in a serious reconsideration of the significance of campus ministry."[55] The following year, regional conferences were held throughout the country for campus ministers, students, and university members to discuss this topic.

The second action was a letter from the bishops to college students, who by now had their own organization, NCSC. After the absence of the student voice since the final National Newman Congress was held in August 1968, on March 13–14, 1982, NCSC was chartered by forty college

---

54 Catholic Campus Ministry Association, Brochure describing certification requirements.
55 Religious Literacy and College Students: The Promise of Campus Ministry, conference proceedings, 2.

and university students from across the United States who gathered at St. Columba's Church in New York City. At this meeting, NCSC was unanimously chosen as the name, and David Keuler, a Boston University student from Wisconsin, was elected the first chairperson. Later that year, the coalition wrote and adopted its vision statement, "Building a Vision: Towards a National Catholic Student Coalition," at its second meeting, which took place in November 6–7, 1982, at Boston University and Boston College.

Regional campus ministry groups began to organize. The coalition was the vision of two individuals: Joe Kirchner, a student from Lehman College in New York City whose parents were largely responsible for starting the NFCCS in the 1930s, and Australian Linda Wirth, the IMCS International team representative. With the help of Fr. Jack Bendik and Fr. Joe Kenna, USCC representative of campus ministry and young adult ministry, the diocesan directors of campus ministry acknowledged their support of the proposal at their annual meeting in Chicago in November 1981 and gave moral support and encouragement for students to organize on local, regional, and national levels.

The NCSC held its first annual conference January 2–6, 1985, at St. Thomas University in Miami Shores, Florida, at the same time the CCMA study week was taking place at Barry University in Miami. One hundred and eighty students from twenty states and eighty-five colleges and universities attended the "Sharing the Vision" conference. At their national team meeting at Georgetown Hotel in Washington, D.C., on January 25–27, 1985, the team decided to create its own publication, which they called *Catholic Collegian*; the first issue was published March 18, 1985.

At the 2003 conference in Albuquerque, New Mexico, NCSC teamed with the Council for Ecumenical Christian Ministry to reflect on the theme "CELEBRATE! Weave Us Together," and in 2007, they partnered again, reflecting on "Waters of Faith: Deltas of Change."

NCSC sent a delegation of twenty-five students to Toronto in July 2002 to celebrate World Youth Day, when Catholics from all over the world joined with Pope John Paul II. The coalition helped organize a university café, an open forum where students could gather for coffee, music, testimonies on justice, and fun. They also helped IMCS, the Canadian Catholic Student Association, in one of the main events focusing on how students could interact with those marginalized by society; they drew close to five thousand people to hear Fr. Jean Vanier, the founder of L'Arche, speak at this event.

The University of Arizona, Tucson, Arizona (1993–2003)

From the cold and wet Northwest, I was assigned to my favorite state—Arizona. After serving for six years at the University of Oregon, I took an assignment as Director of St. Thomas More Catholic Newman Center serving the University of Arizona in Tucson. This was a welcome change, but at the same time it was a challenge, because the enrollment of the university was 35,000 to 38,000 students compared to 18,000 in Eugene. But I was glad to be back in the sunshine. I had the privilege of serving the Newman community for ten wonderful years, which was my longest assignment at one Newman Center.

It is my policy that the first year of a new assignment is for listening and observing. By talking to various members of the community—students, faculty, staff, and permanent community members—one can have a good picture of the programs to continue or eliminate and what new programs need to be introduced to meet the needs of the whole community. I believe that we are a pilgrim church as the Second Vatican Council taught in the Dogmatic Constitution on the Church. As a faith community, we need to look at the signs of the time and move on. We cannot be static.

One of the needs I perceived was to have strong student leadership. Every year the staff took the student leadership team for a three-day retreat in the mountains where staff and students bonded together. At the end of the retreat, there was a lot of excitement and energy. Everyone was ready to go down the mountain and meet the challenges of our ministry.

To build a strong faith community, one of the very first things we did was to establish small faith sharing groups. The first year we started with two groups, which expanded to four by the second semester. The following year, there were twelve, and the year after that, there were more than twenty, mostly led by students. The participants were committed to their respective group for the whole semester and sometimes for the whole academic year. It was very exciting to see the students coming week after week to learn more about their faith, the scriptures, and how to put what they learned into practice in their daily lives.

Faith formation is one of the aspects for campus ministries as outlined in the pastoral letter on campus ministry. To form our students in their faith experience, we offered all different types of retreats—freshmen retreats, undergraduate retreats, confirmation retreats, busy person retreats, young adult and graduate retreats, women's retreats, and Holy Week retreats for those in RCIA. As I said earlier, for some of the students, these retreats were a turning point in their faith journey. Several students became involved in the Newman community while attending the university because of these retreats, and today I know several alumni who are serving their parishes because of their involvement in retreats and ministry at the Center. The Spirit blows where it wills. Besides retreats, bible studies, faith sharing groups, and theological education, I supported the "Science and Theology Forum," a wonderful program that was already established when I arrived in Tucson in which a variety of speakers spoke about the relationship between science and theology. This program is still going on.

Even though one of the main purposes of a Newman Center is to help the students develop their faith experience while attending the university, other adults choose to be members of the Newman community for a variety of reasons. One adult in his late seventies once told me that he attends Mass at the Newman Center because he is energized in his faith when he sees so many young women and men celebrating Mass together. Most of these adults were our financial backbone. One of my goals was not to have two separate communities but one. So I challenged the permanent community members to be involved in retreats, students' events, liturgy, and social events. Many rolled up their sleeves and got to work. Once a month, we cooked a pasta dinner for the students and the community. These adults did most of the cooking, the serving, the setup, and the cleaning. It was wonderful to see the two communities working hand in hand.

Today all universities have foreign students. In my time in Tucson, the University of Arizona had about two thousand international students. Since I came from another country myself (Malta), I knew from experience how difficult it can be for some to integrate into the community. I was asked to serve on the University Executive Board of the International Friends. The board members helped international students to integrate themselves with the university and the Tucson community. Realizing how many international students attended the Newman Center, two or three times a semester we had an international Mass followed by an international pot-luck dinner. These Masses and dinners were great experiences not only for the foreign students but also for the Americans. Various languages were used for the readings, prayers, and songs at the Mass. Every international Mass reminded me of Pentecost.

Wherever I served, I always promoted social justice, and I always found the communities very receptive. In Tucson, we had a regular group that went *every week to a Catholic Worker house to feed the homeless. Once a month, I celebrated Mass at the Catholic Worker house under a shed. Whether I celebrated Mass under the shed or in a cathedral, I felt the presence of Jesus just the same. During the winter, the Newman Center joined other congregations to offer housing to homeless people. Once a week fifteen to twenty men would come for dinner and to sleep over. Students and others helped prepare the dinner and breakfast, while other students stayed at the Center all night in case of some emergency. For me it was quite a learning experience to listen to these men as I and the staff shared dinners with them. Social justice experiences had an impact on three students who opened Maggie's Place, a house for pregnant women in Phoenix a few years after they graduated from U of A; later, they expanded their ministry to Idaho and Minnesota.*

Alternative Spring Break was another social justice event that took place each year. Students had tremendous experiences as they served the needy in the Los Angeles area or on reservations in Arizona and New Mexico. It was a joy for me to see the students helping many children in their classrooms or painting an old person's home or a whole school. The interaction between our students and the people on the reservation was invaluable. These social justice experiences were a teaching moment for many students and the staff. For some, it was a life-changing one.

One of the highlights of my tenure in Tuscon was the visit to the Newman Center by Nigerian Cardinal Francis Arinze who came to visit the African priests who ministered in the Diocese of Tucson. Cardinal Arinze was the President of the Vatican's Pontifical Council on Inter-Religious Dialogue. While visiting the African priests, the cardinal requested to visit the Catholic Center at U of A. So on April 12, 2001, Tucson Bishop Manuel Moreno brought Cardinal Arinze to the Center. After having a tour of the Center and chatting with me about our ministry to the university, especially the students, the cardinal had a lively conversation with the African students while we served lunch. The cardinal was very impressed that on such short notice, more than 80 African students and others attended the event.

Every morning I went for a walk around the campus mall. On September 11, 2001, as I returned from the walk, the plant manager, David Silvestri, told me to turn on the television because he heard on the news that an airplane went through one of the World Trade Towers in New York. A few minutes after I turned on the television, I saw the second plane going through the second tower. I thought I was watching a movie. I could not believe what I was witnessing. I was in shock. Around 7:15 a.m., the administrative assistant of University of Arizona President Peter Likins called me to tell me that Dr. Likins would like all of the campus ministers to join him at a noon service on the campus mall to memorialize this tragic event. Thousands of people came together on the mall—some were in shock, others were angry, and still others were frustrated. That day, our two Masses (at 12:05 p.m. and 5:15 p.m.) were packed. Additionally, the students organized an evening candlelight prayer vigil that took place on the lawn in front of the Newman Center. About three hundred fifty people attended. As I reflected on the Mass attendance on the day of the tragedy and the weekend after, I thought how sad it was that people would come to Mass only when they faced a crisis. I wish our churches would be packed every Sunday.

Another incident that brought the university community together was the shooting of three professors in the Nursing Department. A student, apparently angry over being barred from taking exams, shot three professors and turned the gun on himself in front of a number of students. As I heard of the incident, I called the Nursing Department to offer any assistance that the Newman Center staff could offer. I attended the memorial service that was held at the university, and the Newman Center held a special Mass for the three professors. A few days after the incident, when the department was ready to open again, the Dean of the Nursing Department asked me to bless the premises before classes resumed. I was impressed by the number of faculty, staff, and administrators who took part in the blessing of the whole building, including the classroom where the incident happened. The Nursing Department appreciated my willingness to bless the building.

I have always felt it is my responsibility as a director to take good care of the property and to make needed improvements. On one occasion, when we had an international gathering in the basement of the Center, six students could not join us because they were wheelchair bound. At that moment, I told the members of our community that we needed to install an elevator so that the whole building would be accessible by everyone. I was surprised that within a few weeks I had all the money needed to install the elevator. Another needed improvement was chapel lights; the chapel was too dark. People told me over and over that we needed better lighting in the chapel. Once again, I made an appeal to the community, and new fixtures were installed to improve the lighting in the chapel.

The last thing I did at the Center was to install stained glass windows at all the entrances of the chapel. This project was completed as part of our commemoration of the 75th anniversary of the foundation of the Newman community on the campus of the University of Arizona and as a tribute to *me as I ended my ten years as director. All the proceeds went toward the establishment of a scholarship fund in my name to be used to help students attending retreats or attending the university.*

FINANCES AND CAMPUS MINISTRY

One of the main worries of campus ministers has been money—where they would find the funds they needed to sustain and maintain their programs. Throughout the history of campus ministry, diocesan subsidies and budgets have been cut or maintained. Thus in 1979, Fr. Leo Piguet, pastor at St. Thomas Aquinas Center at Purdue University in West Lafayette, Indiana, edited *Fund Raising: A Primer for Campus Ministers*, published by the National Institute for Campus Ministries, a non-profit organization that supports Catholic and Jewish ministries in higher education. Likely the first book addressing the issue of campus ministry and finances, *Fund Raising*'s purpose was "to provide a short cut to those campus ministers who realize the only way they can assure their future of ministry for themselves and their institution is to raise at least part of the money themselves."[56] The book attempted to teach others "how to"—how to get started, how to raise money from parents, how to develop committed alumni, how to help students become donors, and so forth. Fr. Piguet may have been the first one to argue that fund raising and development is a ministry and not a chore.

In recent years, the need to raise funds for campus ministry sites has been more acute. What happened in the '70s was now being repeated in the '90s. With little or no financial support from local dioceses, it became evident that many directors or pastors of university Catholic centers had to raise money in order to administer and maintain their facilities and to promote the wonderful programs offered to the university communities. As a response to this need, CCMA sponsored the first Development Institute that took place at John Paul II Newman Center at the University of Illinois in June 1997. With the help of professional fund raisers and development directors and consultants, this institute equips campus ministers for their development and fund-raising efforts and techniques. The annual institute has helped hundreds of campus ministers and development directors to see the spiritual aspect of development and

---

56 Leo Piguet, ed., *Fund Raising: A Primer for Campus Ministers* (National Institute for Campus Ministries, 1979) 7.

fund raising. Additionally, two alumni—Peter de Keraty, who served as development director at St. Mary's Catholic Center at Texas A&M University, and John Flynn, who served as the director of institutional advancement at the St. Lawrence Catholic Center at the University of Kansas—founded Petrus Development in order to seek and empower organizations to create and sustain effective fund development programs. They focus mainly on Catholic ministry in higher education.

COOPERATION AMONG
THE THREE MAJOR ORGANIZATIONS

Over the past decade, the three major organizations of campus ministry—CCMA, NADDCM, and NCSC—have enhanced their cooperative efforts. On November 14, 1999, the three organizations hosted the first annual reception for the U.S. bishops at the Hyatt Regency on Capitol Hill. Approximately sixty-five bishops attended the reception. Seven campus ministry programs received awards recognizing their exemplary work in one of the six aspects of campus ministry as well as one vocations program. A year later, the three organizations co-sponsored a national convention, "Open Minds and Open Hearts to Christ: Jubilee 2000," to celebrate the Great Jubilee and the future of the Catholic Church in the Third Millennium. They gathered December 28, 2000–January 1, 2001, at the Galt House Hotel and Suites in Louisville, Kentucky.

Through the efforts of USCCB's Assistant Secretary for Higher Education and Campus Ministry Msgr. John Strynkowski, a joint meeting of CCMA, NADDCM, and NCSC took place in Washington, D.C., on November 15, 2000. The meeting's purpose was to examine ways the three could work together toward a common front. Another joint effort was in November 2001, when the three organizations recognized for the first time a bishop who actively supported campus ministry in his diocese; Bishop Walter F. Sullivan of the Diocese of Richmond was the first recipient.

Organizations have a tendency to become stagnant. At those times, the leaders of the organizations need to evaluate what is happening and see with a new lens. Both NADDCM and CCMA went through periods of self-evaluation. In light of the fact that the number of diocesan directors was decreasing, NADDCM decided to restructure. In 1998, with the help of a consultant, the leadership was redefined. Now NADDCM has three standing committees with an appointed chairperson heading each committee, while a three-member administrative board elected by the membership oversees the organization.

CCMA also went through a self-evaluation in 1999 and 2000. The executive board, after consultation with the members at large, adopted short- and long-range plans for the total membership. After intensive self-study, the following standing committees were established: Church Relations, Formation and Education, Higher Education Relations, Member Services, Certification and Internal Management, and Development. Ongoing committees are formed as other needs arise. These short- and long-range plans are reviewed on an ongoing basis so that the CCMA executive board can respond to new needs of the members as they arise.

The three organizations are very active in the church today. New trends are emerging nationally in campus ministry, such as parish-based campus ministry; the increase in non-ordained campus ministers; the responsibility of one person to minister to various colleges and universities; the closing of campus ministry sites as new ones are established or new centers are built; the role of students serving as peer ministers on staff; and the appointment of lay men, lay women, and religious as directors for both local campus ministries and as diocesan directors.

The bishops concluded in "Empowered by the Spirit" that campus ministry "is vitally important for the future of the Church and society."[57] Recognizing the importance of campus ministry in state institutions, one wonders what impact Catholic campus ministry has had on the beliefs and worship practices of students involved in Newman Centers over the past few decades. In order to find the answer, the Subcommittee for Campus Ministry of the USCCB commissioned a study in 2001 from CARA. Published in the fall of 2005, the survey revealed, among other things, that "among self-identified Catholics who attended college or university for some period of time, those who participated in campus ministry are more likely than those who did not to 1) attend Mass at least once a month, 2) register in a parish, 3) be very involved in parish or other religious activities, 4) donate money to a Catholic parish or another Catholic organization, 5) help the needy as [an essential part] of their

---

57 NCCB, Empowered by the Spirit, par. 103.

faith, 6) encourage someone to serve as a priest, sister or brother."[58] The study presented some important differences in current religious attitudes and behaviors between those who participated in campus ministry in college and those who did not.

These surveys have shown the importance of campus ministry for students attending state colleges or universities. This has been reiterated by Fr. William Byron, S.J., after the massacre that took place at Virginia Polytechnic Institute and State University (Virginia Tech) on April 16, 2007. In his article, "Reflections on Virginia Tech: Is There Any Defense Against Malice?", Fr. Byron states that "campus ministry is as important as the counseling center on a college campus. The physical attractiveness and proximity of Catholic ministry facilities to the students is important." He continues, "Certainly, psychological trauma requires immediate attention, but so does the stress of faith and the strain on spirituality. Moreover, the power of faith and religion to ready the human spirit to withstand any assault, physical or psychological, cannot be overestimated." That's why, he concludes, "The Church has to provide this ministry in campus settings that are not Catholic."[59]

Even Pope John Paul II, in a gathering of young people at the Kiel Center in St Louis on January 26, 1999, recognized the importance of campus ministry when he encouraged them to be children of the light. He urged them to attend "your parishes, religious instruction in your high school and colleges, in your youth groups and **Newman Centers**" so that they could come to know as much as they can about Christ who is their light.[60]

The words printed in the booklet for the 1968 National Student Congress held at Rutgers University/Douglass College Campus in New Brunswick, New Jersey sums up the history of the Movement: "We have come from meager beginnings to a bright and promising future. We are grateful to many especially those who have seen our dreams and in many instances made them real."[61] "In our vision," the bishops wrote in their pastoral letter, "campus ministry, empowered by the Spirit, faces a future bright with promise."[62]

---

58 CARA, *The Impact of Catholic Campus Ministry on the Beliefs and Worship Practices of U.S. Catholics* (Washington, DC: Center for Applied Research in the Apostolate, 2005).

59 Catholic News Service, 18 April 2007.

60 Pope John Paul II. Address to the youth at Kiel Center in St. Louis, 26 January 1999.

61 Rev. Jack Bendick, Keynote address, 6 January 1988.

62 NCCB, Empowered by the Spirit, par.105.

University of Nevada, Las Vegas (2004 to the present)

After ten years as Newman Center director at the University of Arizona, I took a one-year sabbatical. I spent ten days in Maryland with U of A alumni while visiting several Smithsonian museums and experiencing the Fourth of July in Washington, D.C. Then I joined thirty-eight Dominican friars and sisters on a pilgrimage to the lands of Dominic. It was a memorable pilgrimage and very moving to be at the places where our Order had its beginning and to be in the cities where St. Dominic lived and preached. After the pilgrimage, I spent time with my family before my sister and I went on a tour of Australia, New Zealand, Singapore, and Indonesia. I also visited England twice—once to go to see my favorite soccer team, Arsenal, play a couple of matches, and the other to visit friends in Manchester. While there I went to visit Birmingham, Oxford, and Littlemore—important sites related to the life of Blessed John Henry Cardinal Newman. Then I spent few more months with my family before I returned to the United States.

My plans were to be an associate director at some Newman Center. But I have always felt that my ministry has been directed by the words from the prophet Isaiah:"My thoughts are not your thoughts and my ways are not your ways" (55:8).While in Malta, I sent a Christmas e-card to my provincial, Fr. Roberto Corral, O.P. In return, I received a thank you with a proposal to be the director of St. Thomas Aquinas Catholic Newman community serving the University of Nevada, Las Vegas. After prayerful consideration, I accepted the assignment. I felt God still gave me the energy to minister to a new community, albeit a much smaller one than the previous ones.

The Newman Center was located in an interfaith building built in 1974. The Protestants had left before I came in 2004 because they did not have enough people to support their ministry. A couple of years after I became director, Hillel, the Jewish organization on campus, left because they felt the need to have their own place. So the interfaith building, which is owned by the Diocese of Las Vegas, officially became the Newman Center. With this move, more space was available and we could hire more peer ministers. Additionally, we were able to have a Blessed Sacrament chapel for daily Mass and for people to come and pray.

One of the dreams that the community had, even before I arrived in Las Vegas, was to build a chapel and a Newman Center on campus. We have the land, which is a blessing. The previous directors made some plans to fulfill this dream. When I took over, one of the main goals was to start a capital campaign for a new building. My associate director, David Zeamer, accepted the responsibility of serving as development director. We launched the campaign in October 2007 on the feast of Our Lady of the Rosary, under whose patronage we are conducting our campaign. In the last couple of years, I went to several parishes at the invitation of the pastors to preach about our vision and to take up second collections. We have received tremendous support from these parishes. We still have a long way to go, but I believe in God's providence. God will provide all our needs.

I still enjoy working with the students and the university community. Through advertising and the hard work of the peer ministers, we are able to attract more students to the Center. Students have been involved in the running of the Center under the guidance of David Zeamer and me. They lead the music ministry, bible studies, weekly praise and worship, retreats, social activities, and social justice events. To promote social justice issues in the city, our social justice peer minister holds a "Social Justice Awareness Museum" each semester in order to help the community become familiar with the many agencies that serve the Las Vegas area.

Wherever I served, I have always felt that the student peer ministers were very valuable. It is not different at UNLV. As students take ownership, they realize their responsibilities and so mature in their ministry and faith. My joy is that several students who were involved in the various Newman Centers where I have had the privilege to serve are now very much involved in their parishes. As one alumnus told me, he tasted ministry at the Newman Center and now he wants to continue ministering in his faith community as a permanent deacon in addition to teaching at a community college.

I do not know how long I will be at UNLV—after all, I am getting up in years—but God has blessed me with good health even after I had open heart surgery on November 29, 2005. Praise God that I recovered very quickly and was able to resume my ministry. I still go to the gym and play racquetball. God has been good to me in all these years as a priest and campus minister. On April 2, 2010, I celebrated my fiftieth anniversary of my ordination to the priesthood. Over these years, I have learned a lot from my colleagues in campus ministry, my priest friends, and the laity that I worked with. I have been able to give in return, nationally, regionally, and locally.

ACKNOWLEDGMENTS

The author gratefully acknowledges the following individuals who contributed to the completion of this book: Dr. Jeff Burns; Fr. Jack Bender; Br. Raymond Bertheaux, O.P.; Dr. Michael Galligan-Stierle; Dr. Don McCrabb; Chrysta Bolinger; Fr. Jim Bacik; Bishop Phillip Straling; Ms. Dorothy Gee; and Mr. Johnson Shao, an alumnus of the University of Nevada, Las Vegas, and the St. Thomas Aquinas Newman Center.

Special thanks to Ms. Carrie Powell, an alumna of the University of Arizona and the St. Thomas More Newman Center, who read and edited this manuscript. I am very grateful for her time and suggestions.

ABBREVIATIONS

CARA	Center for Applied Research in the Apostolate
CCMA	Catholic Campus Ministry Association
CSAA	Catholic Student Association of America
FCCC	Federation of Catholic College Clubs
IMCS	International Movement of Catholic Students
NADDCCM	National Association of Diocesan Directors of Catholic Campus Ministry
NCEA	National Catholic Educational Association
NCMA	National Campus Ministry Association
NCSC	National Catholic Student Coalition
NCWC	National Catholic Welfare Council
NFCCS	National Federation of Catholic College Students
NNCA	National Newman Chaplains' Association
USCC	United States Catholic Conference

BIBLIOGRAPHY

Archives of the Archdiocese of Milwaukee

Archives of the Archdiocese of San Francisco

Archives of the Dominicans of the Western Province

Cleary, Donald, ed. *Newman Club Federation: A Manual for Newman Leaders*. May 12, 1942.

Crews, Clyde F. *American and Catholic: A Popular History of Catholicism in the United States*. Cincinnati, OH: St. Anthony Messenger Press, 2004.

Evans, John Whitney. *The Newman Movement: Roman Catholics in American Higher Education, 1883–1971*. Notre Dame, IN: University of Notre Dame Press, 1980.

Galligan-Stierle, Michael, ed. *The Gospel on Campus: A Handbook of Campus Ministry Programs and Resources*, 2nd ed. Washington, DC: The United States Catholic Conference, 1996.

Harrington, Timothy. 1921. Memories of the early days of the oldest Newman Club. *Newman Quarterly*, summer.

Kasdorf, Bill, and Phil Haslanger, *Aggiornamento: St. Paul's University Chapel*. Madison, WI: The University Catholic Center, 1974.

Leege, David. *Catholics and the Civic Order: Parish Participation, Politics, and Civic Participation*. Notre Dame, IN: Notre Dame Study of Catholic Parish Life, 1988.

McCrabb, Donald, ed. *Religious Literacy and College Students: The Promise of Campus Ministry*. CCMA, 1995.

Minutes and newsletters of NNCA and CCMA from 1969—1972

National Newman Club Federation. *National Newman Club Manual*, 5th ed. 1962.

Notes from Fr. Jack Bender, chaplain of the Newman Club Federation

Shaw, P. Gerard, ed. *Empowered by the Spirit: Campus Ministry Faces the Future: A Commentary*. North Andover, MA: Merrimack College Press, 1986.

Wisconsin Magazine of History, Vol. 54, No. 3, Spring 1971.

CCMA EXECUTIVE BOARD CHAIRPERSONS

1969–70	Rev. Charles Forsyth, OSB
1970–72	Rev Raymond Sullivan
1972–73	Rev. Kean Cronin
1973–75	Rev. Patrick O'Neill, OSA
1975–76	Rev. John Marshall
1976–77	Bro. Cosmas Rubencamp, CFX
1977–78	Ms. Jennifer Konecny
1978–79	Dr. Robert Ludwig
1979–80	Mr. Steve Zientek
1980–83	Rev. George M. Schroeder
1983–84	Ms. Christine M. Rossi
1984–87	Rev. Raymond Lagesse, SJ
1987–89	Sr. Brenda Gonzales, SCN
1989–91	Mr. Pat Corcoran
1991–92	Ms. Marty Woodword
1992–93	Rev. Bob Lord
1993–96	Rev. Sean Cooney
1996–97	Sr. Joanne Sullivan
1997–2001	Mr. Pete Morgan
2001–02	Rev. J. Friedel
2002–03	Ms. Mary Matunis
2003–07	Ms. Dee Bernhardt
2007–09	Rev. Nathan Castle, OP
2009–11	Mr. Jeff Klein
2011–present	Ms. Laurie Svatek

NATIONAL CONVENTION LOCATIONS

1989	New Orleans, LA
1992	San Jose, CA
1995	Atlanta, GA
1998	Austin, TX
2000	Louisville, KY
2003	Orlando, FL
2005	San Antonio, TX
2007	San Diego, CA
2009	Atlanta, GA
2011	Clearwater, FL

CATHOLIC CAMPUS MINISTRY ASSOCIATION AWARDS

Since 1974, CCMA has been awarding various awards to campus ministers who served the ministry locally, regionally and nationally.[63] The first award was named after **Rev. Charles Forsyth**, who served as the transitional president between the National Chaplains' Association and the forming of the Catholic Campus Ministry Association. It is given to a campus minister who demonstrates outstanding leadership in campus ministry on the local, regional, and national levels. The first recipient of this most prestigious award was Rev. Charles Forsyth, O.S.B., in 1974.

Another award, given to a person or groups who have provided outstanding encouragement and support to campus ministry or the Association, is the **Archbishop Paul J. Hallinan** award. Archbishop Hallinan served as Newman Chaplain to the Catholic students at Western Reserve University in Cleveland, Ohio. The National Newman Chaplains' Association established the Archbishop Paul Hallinan Award. In 1977 CCMA reclaimed the award.

Exemplary Program awards are presented to campus ministry programs and activities that best exemplify in the six aspects of campus ministry as described in the bishops' pastoral letter, "Empowered by the Spirit," and vocation ministry. The honor is awarded to the campus ministers and their ministries for outstanding programming in campus ministry.

In November 2001, the **Exemplary Bishop Award** was given for the first time. Many bishops throughout the country support and encourage campus ministry in their dioceses. Each year at the USCCB's fall meeting of bishops, CCMA hosts a breakfast gathering of Catholic bishops to engage them in discussions on matters of high importance to the continued growth of Catholic campus ministry across the country. The award is presented at this breakfast to a bishop, nominated by his campus ministers, for his unwavering support to the advancement of Catholic campus ministry.

The Exemplary Administrator Award was created in 2008 by the Higher Education Relations Committee. Campus ministers nominate qualified administrators of colleges and universities who are extremely

---

63 This information taken from the CCMA Website (www.ccmanet.org).

helpful to campus ministry, who consistently go the "extra mile" to further the mission of Catholic campus ministry in higher education.

The latest award was established in 2011. The Rev. **Msgr. Vincent Krische Award** for excellence in Catholic campus ministry development was created in honor of Msgr. Krische for his lifelong contributions to fundraising and development for Catholic campus ministry. This award is presented to the person who has made identifiable impact or contributions to the field of development in Catholic campus ministry in higher education. Msgr. Krische was the first recipient of this award. It was given to him at the Development Institute at the University of Nevada Las Vegas, in June 2011.

THE ARCHBISHOP PAUL HALLINAN AWARD

1977	The Catholic Church Extension Society
1979	Rev. Patrick H. O'Neill, OSA
1982	Saint Xavier College, Chicago
1984	Sr. Margaret M. Ivers, IBVM
1987	NCCB Campus Ministry Pastoral Letter Committee, Most Rev. William Friend, Chair
1989	Rev. Vincent E. Krische and the St. Lawrence Catholic Campus Center
1990	George J. Goudreau
1992	University of Dayton
1993	Missouri State Knights of Columbus
1994	Frank J. Lewis Foundation
1995	Rev. James J. Bacik
1996	Dr. Donald R. McCrabb
1998	Most Rev. Patrick F. Flores
2000	Rev. Robert J. Lord
2001	Most Rev. John J. Leibrecht
2002	Thomas J. Donnelly
2004	Most Rev. John McCarthy
2005	Timothy A. Garry
2006	Michael Galligan-Stierle
2008	Mary Matunis
2010	Msgr. J. Patrick Keleher